You Can Do It!

Carl Mays

BROADMAN PRESS
NASHVILLE, TENNESSEE

4282-48 (BRP)
4252-51
ISBN: 0-8054-5251-6

Dewey Decimal Classification: 248.4
Subject heading: CHRISTIAN LIFE

Unless otherwise indicated the Scripture quotations are taken from *The Living Bible, Paraphrased* (TLB) (Wheaton: Tyndale House Publishers, 1971).

Quotations marked:

KJV are taken from the King James Version.

Phillips are taken from *The New Testament in Modern English*, © J. B. Phillips, 1958. Used with permission of the Macmillan Company.

ASV are taken from the American Standard Version.

Library of Congress Catalog Card Number: 76-59509
Printed in the United States of America

Dedicated to
my parents
Hildred and Perry Mays

To write Carl Mays or to inquire about “You Can Do It!” seminars, address Creative Ministries, P.O. Box 266, Gatlinburg, Tennessee, 37738.

Introduction

Stories, books, dramas, and other forms of communication usually spring from ideas planted through personal experiences. The idea for this particular book was conceived one evening when I attended an area premiere of my musical drama, *The Clown.*

Nervous before and during the performance but confident in the cast's abilities and in their dependence upon the Lord, I was elated with the response which came at the conclusion of the presentation. When the audience was dismissed, I made my way to the stage to congratulate the cast and to thank them for a job well done. It was near the stage that a woman came by to speak with me.

The woman told me how much she enjoyed and benefited from *The Clown.* I thanked her for her gracious comments. As she continued to talk, the woman told me that her church had presented a couple of my dramas—*Celebration: A Writer in Search of a Play* and *Playing Church.* The woman said that they had meant much to her and the other church members. Again, I thanked her for her gracious comments—for sharing with me the words always welcomed by a writer. Then, however, she got to the nitty-gritty of what she had really come forward to say.

"But Carl," she tacked on to the end of a comment, "I wish you would write a book for us. Write a book that is happy and entertaining like your dramas—a book that glorifies Christ and celebrates real victory in life—a book we can read in our homes when the drama is over and the lights have been turned off in the auditorium."

When I returned to my motel room later that evening, I thought seriously of what the woman had proposed. Prior to that encounter, I had been considering "getting started" on an experiential book of some sort. I had been praying about it, asking God to lead me in the direction I should go.

That night, in my motel room, I began jotting down ideas for the book. As the ideas came then and continued to flow on my plane flight home the next day, I realized it would be a book about "real-life drama." It would be a book about people searching for and finding glorious victory through Jesus Christ. I pray that you might enjoy and benefit from this book and that God might use it to increase your happiness and your awareness of his Son.

Carl Mays

Contents

"This is God's message . . .
Not by might,
nor by power,
but by my spirit,
says the Lord of Hosts
—you will succeed
because of my Spirit"

ZECHARIAH 4:6, TLB

1/You Can Do It!

You can do it . . .
You can do it . . .
We know you can do it!

You can do it . . .
You can do it . . .
We know you can do it!

The championship game of the state high school basketball tournament was rushing to a dramatic close. With time-out called, fourteen seconds showed on the overhead scoreboard clock. The underdog team, clad in red and white sweat-soaked uniforms, huddled around their coach on the sidelines. They squirted water in their mouths and wiped their faces with towels as they listened intently to instructions. The hometown crowd, sparked by energetic cheerleaders, urged the boys on to a victorious upset.

Going into the fourth quarter, the hometown team had been trailing by twelve points. But now they had valiantly surged from behind to cut the deficit to a single point, 78-79. The excitement of their momentum radiated like electricity throughout the packed and noisy gymnasium.

The buzzer sounded time in. The boys clasped hands, gave a determined shout for victory, and ran back onto the court.

Following their coach's strategy, they set up an often-practiced full-court press. The other team had their plans carefully formulated also. They had possession of the ball when play resumed, and the inbounds pass found its desired target. The opposition moved the ball across the center line with nine seconds remaining in the game.

Then, suddenly, a double-team trap forced a bad pass that was alertly picked-off by a hometown player. Five seconds flashed on the clock as the boy now dribbled back across the center line. A teammate broke for the basket, and the boy who had stolen the ball flipped it to him. The player caught the ball without breaking stride, dribbled twice, went up for the goal, and bounced the ball against the backboard. The buzzer sounded and the ball dropped through the net as the game ended: 80-79!

The taste of victory was sweet!

The victory gained by that team made the price they had paid worthwhile. The months and years of practice, the dedication, and discipline, resulted in outstanding dividends.

Comparatively speaking, few of us ever have the opportunity to be an integral part of such an athletic victory. We do have a fantastic opportunity, however, to claim the real, more meaningful, day-by-day victories that life has to offer. All of us have this opportunity, but so few of us ever claim it. So few of us experience real victory in our lives.

If you are one of the many who has never tasted the sweetness of real victory, you can do it. I know you can. Doing it is what this book is all about. Jesus said, "My purpose is to give life in all its fullness" (John 10:10).

Frustrated Dreams

It was Thoreau who said that most of us live lives of quiet desperation. This desperation, sometimes not so quiet, is the result of personal discontent, unhappiness, and frustrated dreams that never materialize. The desperation shows up in our daily lives as it colors our actions, reactions, and attitudes.

A few years ago I accompanied my son to a hospital for his tonsillectomy. As I sat in the waiting room during the surgery, I was shocked at the sight of a small boy who was rolled down the hall on a stretcher. The child was unconscious. One of his eyes was terribly discolored and swollen. The other eye was in the line of a deep gash which began on his forehead and ran down to his cheek. His puffy lips were split and his misshapen nose was apparently fractured. His body was covered with a white, blood-splattered sheet, and I couldn't see the damage it had received. My initial thought was that the little boy had been struck and dragged some distance by a car or truck.

When I asked an attendant what had happened, I discovered it was not a car or truck that had struck the child. He was attacked by his father! In a blind rage of passion, the father released his pent-up frustrations and anxieties on his son when the boy did not eat all the food which was on his plate at mealtime.

Hard to believe? That's what I thought also. But when I later talked with a nurse about the horrible incident, she told me that such an occurrence was not at all uncommon. She said that the number of such cases was increasing each year.

"Why?" I later asked a psychologist friend of mine. "What causes parents, especially fathers, to beat their children?"

"Anger at themselves, their employers, their marriage partners, or their situations," my friend explained. "This anger builds up and seeks release. The child cannot defend himself; therefore, he becomes the perfect release valve. As a result of some act that displeases the parent, the child becomes a target for the exploding anger and frustration. Usually, with anxiety-laden emotions spent, the parent later is sorry for what he did. That, however, doesn't mean he won't do it again when the frustration and anger builds back up."

The psychologist told me that all the victims of child-beaters do not wind up in a hospital. Some suffer worse punishment, as a result of continued mental and verbal attacks upon their emotions. Young minds become warped. Young lives are emotionally, mentally, and spiritually deformed. They are one product of people who "live lives of quiet desperation."

The effects of other desperate people do not surface so drastically. Some of these people have characteristics similar to the woman who belittles others in an attempt to make herself appear larger, greater, more necessary. Or, there are those who constantly blame other people and circumstances for their own personal failures and frustrations. Then, there are some who fabricate their lives with negative thoughts—like the man in need of a "jack". . . .

The man was driving down a highway when one of the tires on his car had a blowout. He swerved to the shoulder of the highway, got out of the car, and inspected the damaged tire. Then he opened the car's trunk to get the spare. The spare was intact and full of air, but the man soon discovered that his jack was missing. He then recalled that he had used it in his garage at home and had forgot to put it back in the trunk.

In frustration, the man kicked the tire and addressed heaven in blemished prayer. Finally, he remembered the station he had seen along the highway about a mile back. With no other cars in view, he began the hike to the service station. "I'll borrow a jack from them," he said to himself, "and ask one of them to drive me back."

He had gone only a short distance before he started to think, "What if they won't let me borrow their jack?" The more he thought about their possible reaction to his request, the angrier he became. And the angrier he became, the more he thought about it. "If they do let me use their jack, they'll probably charge me five bucks just to drive me back!" he said to himself. "They won't let me borrow the jack," he continued, "but they'll say they'll rent it to me for five dollars!"

"Ten bucks . . . ten bucks, just to borrow their jack and get them to bring me back!" His anger continued to grow, and his frustration at the "miserable, money-hungry animals" who worked at the service station continued to multiply. Then, he sighted the station.

"Who do they think they are?" he asked as he neared his destination and saw a man sitting behind a desk. He was drinking a cup of coffee and reading a newspaper. Drawing closer, the frustrated driver eyed another employee who was involved in servicing a car on a rack. "Wiseacre," the driver erupted under his breath. "Nothing but a money-hungry wiseacre who wants to make a fortune off stranded motorists!"

As the driver stepped onto the pavement in front of the station, the employee who had been working in the service area went inside the station to confer with the man behind the desk. They were talking about a mechanical problem with the car being serviced when the red-faced driver stepped up to the door. The veins in his neck stood out like taut cords and his entire body trembled with anger.

He grasped the door and flung it open. It crunched noisily against the glass window and the two men quickly turned their attention toward the intruder. Wide-eyed, their blank looks met his torrid expression. The driver now stood spread-legged in the doorway, his hands on his hips.

"Keep your jack!" the driver split the momentary static-like silence which had accompanied his banging entrance. "I wouldn't use it if you paid me and took me back in a limousine!"

Through blood-red eyes, he stared at the two shocked men, then turned to leave as abruptly as he had appeared.

With wide eyes and open mouths, the two men looked at one another. They didn't know what to say or what to think, because they had no idea what was going on.

The angry driver disappeared from sight.

The not-so-quiet desperation of the driver is humorous, but it pathetically exemplifies the frequent state of modern man. This is one reason there is so little real communication in our society. The unreasonable "thought-out" action of one person or group cannot be comprehended by another person or group. Thus, our anxieties and frustrations conceive and give birth to offsprings. And the situation worsens.

In the first church where I served as a minister, I recall facing the congregation from the pulpit and seeing faces which appeared to reflect contentment and happiness. But as I grew to know the people behind these faces, I discovered day-by-day turmoils camouflaged by the prim, Sunday masks.

Prior to entering the seminary and going into church-related work, I thought that all "professional religionists" exhibited the epitome of happiness. I thought that all pastors, ministers of music, ministers of education, evangelists, and other Christian workers claimed victory after victory, day after day. The naivety of such thinking was spotlighted when I discovered jealousy, rivalry, and personal unrest among people who are supposed to be leading lay people to victory.

As my eyes were opened, I finally grasped what Erich Fromm meant when he said, "So many people die before they really begin to live."

"Why?" I asked myself as I began to realize how wrong I was in thinking that most people and all Christian workers are victorious. Why are there so few victories?

The logical answer is that the people without victory are people without Christ. But this is not necessarily so. I have personally counseled with many "winless" Christians—people who claim to accept Jesus as Savior and as Lord of their lives. I have also experienced heart-to heart talks with fellow church-related workers who know Christ personally but do not know victory.

The answer is in Christ, but it goes much deeper than saying, "I accept you as Savior and Lord and I want to serve you." Much deeper. Only positive, God-led action can breathe life and meaning into these inanimate words.

I believe that many people are "winless"—that they are not experiencing the sweet taste of victory—because they are not really developing and correctly utilizing the talents God has given them. Many people are wasting God-given gifts. And the most detrimental aspect of this is that they know it.

The height of frustration: You are wasting your life and you know it!

Victory will never be yours just because you have ability or education. You will never be a winner if you rely only on your potentialities. Hundreds of thousands of people have ability and education and potentialities. But these hundreds of thousands of people are still winless people, slowly drowning in the sluggish sea of mediocrity.

Why are these people winless? Why are they mediocre? Why are they surrounded by vague anxieties and guilt feelings? They are, because they have not been motivated enough to strive for worthy goals or set quality ambitions. Goethe made the point succinctly: "The important thing in life is to have a great aim and to possess the aptitude and perseverance to attain it."

Unless you establish a worthy goal—unless you are inspired to accomplish a quality ambition that will make your life count, you will never know victory. But you can do it!

Diamonds in the Rough

We are all diamonds in the rough. But our treasures will never be revealed if the rough diamond is not processed. The red-and-white basketball team had aspirations to win the state tournament. They achieved this goal through dedication, discipline, and work, work, work. When the time came, they revealed their worth. But, as important as it seemed to them, this was only a game. We're talking about *your life* now. How much of the real you has been revealed?

We all have hidden values. The way we cultivate these values and what we achieve in life is not dependent upon outward things, situations, circumstances, or other people. What we make of ourselves depends upon how we develop our personal gifts and talents. We must learn to inspect our weak points and our strong points and react according to what we have and to who we are.

"Your sons and daughters will prophesy; your old men will dream dreams and your young men see visions" (Joel 2:28). You must dream dreams; you must see visions. But in order for the dreams to materialize and the visions to become reality, you must put your efforts—your life—where your mind is.

> "If one advances confidently in the direction of his dreams, and endeavors to live the life which he has imagined, he will meet with a success unexpected in common hours. . . . If you have built castles in the air, your work need not be lost; that is where they should be. Now put the foundations under them."
>
> (Thoreau)

You can do it. With the power of God working through you, you can do it. "The Kingdom of God is within you" (Luke 17:21), and God's creative Spirit can hover over your potentialities, stimulate your motives, and give a definite purpose to your life.

In Matthew Arnold's poem, *Empedocles on Etna,* Empedocles, the Greek philosopher, sits atop a mountain and looks down upon the troubled world below. In a soliloquy, he talks of the frustrations, pains, vague anxieties, and general unrest inherent in the lives of the people below. As he considers how man might rid himself of such griefs, he eventually expresses his conclusion in these lines:

"We would have inward peace But will not look within."

But will not look within. In an attempt to alleviate their frustrations, hundreds of thousands of people seem to look everywhere but within. They seek relief with alcohol, society's liquid, cancerous scab. Drug addicts hopelessly grasp for hope. Others grope for "life-blotters" with a few moments of illicit or perverted sex. Still others acquire money and things or seek fame to erase the unhappiness imprinted upon their lives.

Each of us is created in the image of God. Thus, it stands to reason that the better we know our divine model, the better we know ourselves. Jesus must have had this fact in mind when he said that we should know ourselves and inspect our own lives before judging the lives of others.

Look upon God, and you will be able to look within. Give your life to God, and he will lead you to the truth. Jesus said, "The truth will set you free" (John 8:32)—free to grow and to produce and to be victorious!

Most people live halfhearted lives, constantly treading water and growing short of breath. They become so bogged down with the minute things and the trivial details of life, that they have less and less time for the important things that God has called them to do.

God calls us to rise above the contaminated, frustrating slush of mediocrity. God calls us to have ambitions. He calls us to succeed. The people who answer his call are transformed and are never the same. These people do not merely exist. These people live life to the fullest.

You can do it!

2/Ambition Is A Gift

"In everything you do, put God first, and he will direct you and crown your efforts with success" (Prov. 3:6).

Ambition is a gift from God because God is in the life-changing business. He can take an empty life and transform it into one of fullness. When we open our lives to God, he touches us and gives us new outlooks—different perspectives. Such was the case when I had a conflict with a person who attacked me with words and actions and hurt me deeply. At the time, I felt that I despised and hated the man for what he had done.

"Change this man!" I told God. Did you get that? "Change this man!" I *told* God. But God didn't change the man. *He changed me.* God changed me when I finally quit looking into the mirror of my ego and realized I needed changing more than anyone.

When I turned the situation over to God, he took charge and led me to see the "hateful" man in a new light. God helped me see the man as He saw him. God seemed to say to me, "Hey, Carl . . . Jesus died for that man also." My dislike became concern and my hatred grew into compassion. The man was the same, but I was different. And that made the man different.

Just as God gave me a new perspective which led to the solving of my problem, he can give you a new perspective to assist you in erasing frustrations and anxieties in your life. The world will be the same, but you will be different. And that will make the world different.

A Mighty Touch

I was in the Boy Scouts for a while. I learned to tie all the knots, and I memorized the things I needed to know to become a Tenderfoot. My career in Boy Scouts was short-lived, but there is one experience I still recall.

We were hiking in the woods, learning to correctly use our compasses. I remember asking one of the older, more advanced boys why the needle always pointed north. He looked at me sort of funny-like, shrugged his shoulders, and replied, "Just does—that's all."

"It's been magnetized," my scoutmaster overheard us and entered into the conversation. "They touched the needle with a real strong magnet in the factory, and now it always swings toward the magnetic pole of the North."

We're like that needle. We're just lying around with no definite purpose, no definite direction. Then, God touches us and bam! We begin to get it all together. The human personality has been touched with divine power. Now, we're not merely drifting around. We know where we are going because God is leading us. As he leads us, we come to realize, "The things which are impossible with men are possible with God" (Luke 18:27, KJV).

But only when we are willing to turn our lives over to God—and let him direct our direction—will he magnetize us. It is only when we invite his Holy Spirit to direct every area of our lives that we can develop worthy goals and quality ambitions and come to know the real excitement and joy of the Christian life.

In a way, it would be correct to say that we are human *becomings* rather than human *beings.* God did not create us as "finished products." And only with his guidance from within can we approach the levels of which he knows we are capable. In this respect, life is an ongoing process which continually unfolds exciting new vistas of possible accomplishment. After turning our talents and potentialities back over to the skillful hands of the Creator, after seeking from him a new perspective—a new purpose—we can claim his promises: "Ask, and you will be given what you ask for. Seek, and you will find. Knock, and the door will be opened" (Matt. 7:7). "No mere man has ever seen, heard or even imagined what wonderful things God has ready for those who love the Lord" (1 Cor. 2:9).

God Calls Everybody

Without a doubt, God is calling us to realize victory in our lives. No potter wants to see his pottery relegated to a dusty shelf. No sculptor desires that his sculpture be scrapped upon a garbage heap. No artist longs for his treasured art work to become discarded as worthless junk. The Creator wants only the best for his creation. Thus, he calls us away from the "land of the losers" to the sweet taste of victory.

The word *call* has twenty-six different meanings. One meaning is "to say in a loud tone, shout or announce." Another meaning is "to telephone." It could mean "to name," "to awaken," "to give a signal to," "to stop," and so on down the line. But the word *call,* in the sense to which I am now referring, means: "To summon to a specific duty."

So essentially what I am saying is that the God who created the universe, as recorded in Genesis 1:1—the God who gives life to every living thing, as recorded in Acts 17:25—summons every individual to do a specific thing, to discover and develop his or her inherent talents and potentialities. Every person who *has* lived, every person who *is* living, and every person who *will* live, is called by God.

In a manner of speaking, this call is divided into two categories. First of all, God calls everybody to become a Christian. This makes possible the second aspect: God calls all Christians to turn their lives over to him, completely; to invite him to come into their lives and lead in developing into what his creation has the latency to be.

No matter who you are or what you are, I invite you to personally inspect God's call to you. If you are not a Christian, I pray that you will realize that God is definitely calling you, one of his creations, to become a Christian. If you are already a Christian but not claiming victory in your life, I pray that you might offer God the opportunity to change your perspective—to magnetize you and change your life.

God calls everybody to become a Christian. One biblical basis for this statement is found in Isaiah 45:22: "Let all the world look to me for salvation! For I am God; there is no other." Jesus clarified how one might respond to this universal call when he said: "I am the Way—yes, and the Truth and the Life. No one can get to the Father except by means of me" (John 14:6).

It is clear that God is not calling just a few people to come to him through Christ. He is not calling one particular group or race or sect or nationality to believe in the one true God. God calls everybody.

One may ask, "Why does God call everybody?" The answer is, "Because he is a God of love." We've heard about the wrath of God, the anger of God, caused by people who refuse to accept the fullness of life which is offered to them. But these emotions, which can only be defined in limited human terms and never really understood, are overshadowed by the love of God. Because of this love, he sent his Son, Jesus, to die on the cross so that this universal call might be possible. God does not want any of his "creations" separated from him. But our God is also just and fair. If one does not accept the salvation and relationship offered, the separation is inevitable and the continued frustrations are heavy.

Ralph Waldo Emerson said, "There is a crack in everything God has made." I like that. Figuratively speaking, we can see God stroking his fingers of love over the wet cracks in our lives and making us whole.

When I was in the seminary, my days, Sunday through Friday, began at around 5:30 A.M., and I usually tried to get in bed by midnight each evening. On Saturday mornings when I had a chance to sleep late, I attempted to make a whole morning of it. But, as Robert Burns wrote, "The best laid schemes of mice and men often go astray." And the thing that caused my scheme to go astray was a small boy and his affinity with Saturday morning TV. Through the week, a cannon blast could not arouse him, but some *super Saturday morning hero* had no problem at all.

One particular Saturday morning, with my bedroom door closed, I was realizing the bliss of sleep when a series of commercials allowed my son to pay me a visit. He swung open the door, bounded into my room, leaped up onto my bed, and put an end to any foolish ideas of slumber.

After bouncing up and down on my stomach a few times to make sure I was alive and well, he tossed a question my way which seemed to come from deep left field. "Jesus loves everybody, huh Dad?"

Surprised, gradually coming to life, I replied, "Yeah, son, Jesus does love everybody."

Then he came back with, "Jesus likes to love everybody, huh Dad?"

Once again, I agreed with him.

Continuing, he said, "Jesus doesn't whip mommas and daddies and big boys, huh Dad?"

I threw in another agreement, in the back of my mind wondering what he had broken this time.

Then, to cap it off, he came out with, "Jesus just whips monsters, huh Dad?"

Saturday morning TV.

Later, I thought more seriously about what my son had said. It sounded simple. It is simple. Jesus loves everybody. Because, as my son so capably put it, Jesus likes to love people. No matter who we are—Jesus loves us. He loves me and he loves you. Even monsters . . . .

"When we were utterly helpless with no way to escape, Christ came at just the right time and died for us sinners who had no use for him. Even if we were good, we really wouldn't expect anyone to die for us, though, of course, that might be barely possible. But God showed his great love for us by sending Christ to die for us while we were still sinners" (Rom. 5:6-8).

If you have not yet accepted this love God offers, you can do it right now, even as you read these pages. Such an acceptance will be a step in the right direction in erasing frustrations and vague anxieties in your life. No real victory will ever be yours unless you first know Jesus Christ personally. But you can do it:

1. Recognize and admit the fact that you are separated from God, that you have cracks that you have not asked God to mend with his love. Recognize and admit that you have fallen short of the mark

in failing to realize your potentialities. "When Adam sinned, sin entered the entire human race. His sin spread death throughout all the world, so everything began to grow old and die, for all sinned" (Rom. 5:12).

2. Place your trust and belief in God's Son, Jesus Christ. Trust him to give purpose to your life for now and forever. Believe that through him, unrest and discontent can be conquered. "For God loved the world so much that he gave his only Son so that anyone who believes in him shall not perish but have eternal life" (John 3:16).

3. Confess Jesus Christ as your Savior if you really believe he is and invite him to become Lord of your life. This means confess him publicly, acknowledge him now and daily. Don't be ashamed or embarrassed to tell people and show people that you are a Christian. Don't be afraid of spiritually ignorant friends—or enemies. Instead, find Christ, and then lead them to him. "For it is by believing in his heart that a man becomes right with God; and with his mouth he tells others of his faith, confirming his salvation" (Rom. 10:10).

Instinctively, man has historically believed in and worshiped gods. He has turned this belief and worship toward sun gods, moon gods, gods of love and fertility, gods of war, and others too numerous to mention, in an attempt to find the one true God which can give meaning and purpose to life. Man is incomplete, separated from his Creator, and he cannot find completeness until he finds God.

It was true yesterday, is true today, and will be true tomorrow: happiness, purpose, and a reason for living will never really be yours unless you unite with God through his son Jesus Christ. It is as H. G. Wells said, "Until a man has found God, he begins at no beginning; he works to no end."

The Bible constantly testifies to the fact that God does not want us to experience frustration and anxieties that defeat us daily and slowly kill our highest potentialities. But a gap between God and the people created in his image results in such negative rewards.

Many people, however, continue to refuse to admit their problems exist as a result of their poor relationship with their Creator. They still prefer to blame their problems on society—on other people or circumstances beyond their control. They refuse to respond to the first call of God—the call to mend the break and cross the gap, to reunite the creation with the Creator. But if the remainder of this book is to make any sense at all to the reader, the initial step must be taken.

Claim Your Victory

Timothy was a young man who was trying to find his way around in the Christian life. The apostle Paul, a prisoner at the time, wrote to Timothy to instruct him in things to do that would make his life more meaningful and more of a power for God. We could say that this is a portion of an open letter to all Christians today: "Guard well the splendid, God-given ability you received as a gift from the Holy Spirit who lives within you" (2 Tim. 1:14).

Some of us Christians have had the mistaken idea that God only calls a comparatively few people to serve him—pastors, ministers of music, evangelists, or other church-related workers. True, these are special ways in which to live for God and serve him, but God calls everybody, remember? He is calling you to live a full life and reflect your Creator by being involved in areas in which your individual talents might be best developed and utilized for his glory and your victory. He is calling you to claim a personal victory through Jesus Christ. The apostle Paul emphasized this in another of his letters: "Christ has given each of us special abilities—whatever he wants us to have out of his rich storehouse of gifts. Why is it that he gives us these special abilities to do certain things best? It is that God's people will be equipped to do better work for him, building up the church, the body of Christ, to a position of strength and maturity" (Eph. 4:7,12).

All Christians come together to form one Christian body, working for the glory of the Creator and for personal victory through Jesus Christ. The body consists of pastors, businessmen, businesswomen, teachers, farmers, factory workers, lawyers, loving mothers and fathers, and people in all walks of life who are continually discovering who they are and what they are becoming. To be effective members of this body, we must: "Live life, then, with a due sense of responsibility, not as men who do not know the meaning and purpose of life but *as those who do.* Make the best use of your time, despite all the evils of these days. Don't be vague but grasp firmly what you know to be the will of the Lord" (Eph. 5:15-17, Phillips).

God is calling us to realize happiness, fulfillment, and abundant life. If we listen to and heed this call, we will expand and develop. We will blossom into the richness of life. If we turn a deaf ear toward God, if we refuse to accept his call, we will become empty shells of what we could have been. We will remain frustrated scrub plants without flower or fruitage.

The person who aspires to rise above the mediocre scrub life, who struggles to express his dreams and visions of what can be, claims the victory.

The victorious person is never satisfied with himself because he is continuously raising his goal as he follows God's leadership. He is daily expanding his horizons and obtaining a broader vision, a greater perspective, as his ambition grows in proportion to his achievement.

James Allen said: "A man is not rightly conditioned until he is a happy, healthy, and prosperous being; and happiness, health, and prosperity are the result of a harmonious adjustment of the inner with the outer, of the man with his surroundings."

It all begins when you get a glimpse of your real self. It begins when you see yourself as you are and then see yourself as God intended you to become. When, through the grace of God, you catch this glimpse, nothing and no one but yourself can prevent you from claiming victory in life.

You can do it!

3/The Quality Of Ambition

"Except the Lord build the house, they labor in vain that build it" (Ps. 127:1, KJV)

Some people claim it is wrong to be ambitious; they say ambition is evil. Sallust, the Roman writer, said: "It is the nature of ambition to make men liars and cheats who hide the truth in their hearts, and like jugglers, show another thing in their mouths; to cut all friendships and enmities to the measure of their interest, and put on a good face where there is no corresponding good will."

Sallust accumulated a dishonest financial fortune prior to having a "change of heart" and writing about the evils of ambition. Therefore, he might be categorized as an expert on defining "low quality" ambition, drawing from his personal experience. It was this same "low quality" ambition to which Shakespeare referred: "Fling away ambition. By that sin angels fell. How then can man, the image of his Maker, hope to win by it?"

Richard E. Burton, British professor and author, said: "As dogs in a wheel, or squirrels in a cage, ambitious men still climb and climb, with great labor and incessant anxiety, but never reach the top."

Would it be correct to say, "Knives are evil because with them we can kill"? Knives in the hand of skilled surgeons can save lives. Would it be correct to say, "Pencils are evil because with them we can write profanity and other words that debase and destroy"? Pencils in the hands of skilled writers can be used as instruments of inspiration. Would it be correct to say, "Ambition is evil because it can destroy our peace of mind and even our very lives"? Ambition, forged in the will of God, glorifies Christ and leads us on to victory.

The quality of the ambition makes all the difference. If the quality is low, victory will never be achieved, no matter how great the quantity. If the quality is high, that means the Master Builder has been involved and the plans have the capacity for success.

I sat in my office one day and listened to a financially rich man pour out his anxieties and frustrations. He said that he and his wife threw words at one another but had not really communicated in years. He told me that his children had no respect for him and he knew they only tolerated him because of his money.

"Carl," he said, "I thought I had high goals when I started, but if I did, I sure lost them somewhere down the line. I don't know anybody anymore, not even myself, and I'm a million miles away from God!"

Coming in contact with men and women such as this, I began to see just how much many "successful Christian people" need to discover, or rediscover, God's will for their lives. Based upon my own personal contacts, it appears to me that it might be easier to handle poverty without God than to manage riches without God. Whatever the case, there is misery on both ends of the spectrum when God's absence is evident in the lives of those involved.

In a newspaper I read of two deaths, page one carried a story of a young man who had inherited over six hundred thousand dollars. According to the newspaper account, he committed suicide and left a note saying that he could not find himself. He said that he did not seem to belong anywhere, that he was not his own person. The last page in the paper had a small story about a man who took his own life after he had killed his wife and five children. His brother told police that the man did what he did because he was out of work and could not feed and clothe himself or his family.

One man killed himself because he was hopelessly dangling from a mountain of materialism and apparently ran out of objects to hang onto. The other man killed himself and his family because he saw no other escape from such a meaningless existence. Neither man tasted the sweetness of victory. One man was financially rich, the other was financially poor, but neither was financially successful.

I believe that everyone who seeks, sets, and fulfills quality ambitions through the leadership of God, will obtain financial success—but not necessarily financial riches. There is a vast difference between the two. Some people may be financially rich, such as the man in the counseling session to which I referred, but not financially successful. On the other hand, another person may earn only a fraction of the rich man's income and still succeed financially. How can this be?

The person who knows Christ, the person whose ambitions have been forged and molded in the will of God, finds an inner security and peace when these ambitions are being realized. But the person whose ambitions are in conflict with God's will attempts to find an inner security and peace through material riches. This person is frustrated if he doesn't obtain his goal—he is frustrated if he does.

"The love of money is the first step towards all kinds of sin. Some people have even turned away from God because of their love for it, and as a result have pierced themselves with many sorrows" (1 Tim. 6:10).

Money is not evil. It is the *love* of money—the overwhelming craving for money that leads a person to his downfall. If a person's life theme and major ambition is to obtain great financial riches, he will never find the victory that is at the top of life. God does not lead a person to set such a goal. God realizes quality ambitions are not built around a hungry desire to place material wealth above everything else.

Some poverty-stricken people *love* money more than do some financially rich people. This leads to doubled frustrations. They are frustrated because they live in poverty, and they are frustrated because they cannot reach the money-oriented goals they have set.

At the same time, some financially rich people have complete victory because the material wealth came as "frosting on the cake" as higher quality goals were realized. The material wealth was not the ultimate ambition, but it came as they climbed the ladder of success in reaching ambitions of high quality. God does not promise us great wealth, but this great wealth may be obtained—and enjoyed—if we do not make it our purpose for living, if we do not make it a steam roller that crushes the higher qualities of life.

Of course, love of money is not the only factor that leads people to seek low quality goals. It is not the only factor that leads us to wind up treading water and running short of breath. A desire for recognition and fame causes many of us to get caught up in that murky pool. Self-respect and self-esteem are ingredients that are necessary for personal victory. Self-criticism and self-degradation are weapons that kill all too many talents and abilities. But vanity, conceit, and self-glorification kill people. In the philosophic words of Sir Philip Sidney: "To be ambitious of true honor and of the real glory and perfection of our nature is the very principle and incentive of virtue; but to be ambitious of titles, place, ceremonial respects, and civil pageantry, is as vain as the things which we court."

When I had been in church-related work for a while and had begun to gain some recognition as a writer and speaker, I felt threatened by others who shared similar careers. If I heard another young man speak, I focused on his weaker points rather than majoring on his strong points and attempting to learn from what he had to say. Each dramatic presentation I attended, I did so with a critical eye, subjectively comparing the play with my own work and always determining my ability far superior. Christian writers had to pass my close scrutiny before I would accept the fact they really deserved to be published. Older speakers, dramatists, and writers were not as much a threat, however, since I assumed those older than I were just about over the hill anyway.

At this point in my life, I was living in two worlds and not really enjoying either. There was a conflict between my base attitude and the attitude God wanted me to have. This conflict existed because I adhered to my personal motivations and not to the motivations instilled by God. In an attempt to ease the guilt feelings of the situation, I tried to do a little of each. I had definitely asked God to guide me, but, at times I knowingly disregarded God's leadership. This was costly. It cost me peace of mind and the abundant life to which Jesus refers.

But, thank God, things have changed. This is another area in which the Lord has given me a new perspective. Through the experience, I gained an insight into the difference between self-effort for self's sake and self-effort for God's will. The deeper my faith in God and the stronger my belief in myself and my goals, the more I can let other people be themselves and do their things without my feeling threatened by them.

Not long ago I had several meaningful talks with a young minister of music who had been experiencing the "two-world" syndrome that I once faced. Jealousy and envy clung to the goals he had set for himself. He liked to see other choirs make mistakes; one of his prime enjoyments was to hear a "competitive" voice crack or hit a wrong note. Inwardly, he rejoiced and boosted his own ego, while outwardly he wore a smug mask of concern and compassion for the one who faltered.

I pray daily for an older pastor who feels threatened by any minister under forty who gets close to his pulpit. I pray for a high school teacher who feels she is competing with younger teachers just out of college.

Personal ambition outside of God's will has a way of conflicting with a commitment to Christ and with all he represents. Such a misplaced ambition, such a desire to outshine others and stroke our egos at the expense of others, will destroy any chance we might have for personal victory.

I know a woman who has a very nice house. She and her husband are influential in their community, and the children are a credit to the family. But she receives little enjoyment from these blessings because she is so concerned with what other people have and with what other people are doing.

Oh, the number of unhappy, frustrated people who have literally "spent" their lives trying to keep up with someone else. And they have not joined in the competiveness to please themselves as much as they have done it to please others—to make sure that others can see what they are doing. "Am I now seeking the favor of men, or of God? or am I striving to please men? if I were still pleasing men, I should not be a servant of Christ" (Gal. 1:10, ASV).

When we seek God's leadership, and through Christ establish quality goals, we will learn that what other people achieve takes nothing away from us and what we achieve takes nothing away from them. We are not competing with one another, we are competing with base, uncultivated ambitions. Such ambitions are born of Satan rather than of God: "We are not fighting against people made of flesh and blood, but against persons without bodies—the evil rulers of the unseen world, those mighty satanic beings and great evil princes of darkness who rule this world; and against huge numbers of wicked spirits in the spirit world (Eph. 6:12).

Satan would like nothing better than to have us to keep our eyes upon ourselves and others as we turn away from Christ. However, committed Christians do not place themselves in the center of the universe. Such placement, such egocentricity, is the sin the apostle Paul referred to when he wrote: "These men deliberately forfeited the truth of God and accepted a lie, paying homage and giving service to the creature instead of to the Creator" (Rom. 1:25, Phillips).

And this is what *sin* really is: a defiant, self-centered attitude; it is the serving of self, the disregarding of others and God; it is mocking the principles for which Christ died.

It has been said that no one ever really lives until he has found something worth dying for. We can never really experience the joys of victory until the cause of God and the principles of Christ become more important than our lives. Worthy ambitions are set beyond ourselves and are greater than ourselves. Jesus made this clear when he said: "If you insist on saving your life, you will lose it. Only those who throw away their lives for my sake and for the sake of the Good News will ever know what it means to really live" (Mark 8:35).

A Change for the Better

In this chapter, I have told of those who are financially rich and those who are financially poor. But material "success" or the lack of it seems to have little bearing upon the high degree of suffering, unhappiness, and loneliness found in the lives of people who have discovered no worthy reason for their existence.

These people search in just about every possible crevice to find victory, but it eludes them. It escapes through their fingers because they have not turned their search inward and upward. They have not looked at themselves and at God—really looked. If you are a "they"—if your ambitions are out of focus or of low quality or nonexistent, "Be a new and different person with a fresh newness in all you do and think" (Rom. 12:2).

It is not a question of whether or not you *can* change. The question is, "Do you *want* to change?" If your motivation is strong enough, it will happen.

Even though you may be drowning in the strength-sapping clutches of frustrations and anxieties, it is still difficult for you to admit your ambitions are wrong. It's a blow to your ego. That is why, even though you know you are unhappy, you don't want to admit you've been wrong. You don't want to admit that you've wasted a part or a majority of your life. That's why people continue struggling along in slush, rather than confess there is a need for change and then take steps to bring about that change.

Nietzsche, the German philosopher, claimed that before a person can become "more good" he must become "more evil." Nietzsche meant that a person must recognize the evil in himself before the potential good can become an effective force in his life. You can recognize your evil goals and ambitions if you will compare them with what God would have you to really do.

In the famous "closet scene" of Shakespeare's *Hamlet*, Hamlet says to his mother, the queen: "Come, come and sit you down. You shall not budge, You go not till I set you up a glass (mirror) Where you may see the inmost part of you."

The queen in reply said: "O Hamlet, speak no more. Thou turn'st mine eyes into my very soul, And there I see such black and grained spots As will not leave their tinct."

What Hamlet actually forced his mother to look at was not a "glass" (mirror), but a small picture of his murdered father, in which his mother began to see herself implicated in that murder.

You can see yourself as you are and as you have the potential to become by looking into the face of Jesus Christ. Look into his face through Bible study and prayer and personal experience. The more you look into the face of Jesus, the more you will see your own evil and will seek a change in your life. If you will look into this *mirror,* you will be able to share a testimony similar to the one a businessman shared with me not long ago.

"Carl," he began seriously, "I thought I knew more than God knew." He smiled and shook his head. "But I was a fool," he continued. "I thought I had the answers to everything, but come to find out—I didn't even know the questions!"

He went on to tell me that he thought he had all the joy he could have. "I thought *happiness* was blown up all out of proportion," he said. "I didn't think any *happy* people were as *happy* as they claimed to be." He looked at me and sort of smiled again. "Understand?" he asked.

I nodded my head. I understood exactly.

He continued. "One day, though, in a Sunday School class, we were talking about Abraham and about how he gave up one life-style and began anew in an entirely different country. Abraham thought he had joy and satisfaction in his present position, but when he followed God's leadership, he discovered the real meaning of joy and satisfaction. 'Get thee out of thy country' (Gen. 12:1, KJV), God told Abraham, and that's what he did."

The man paused and eyed me carefully, then picked up where he left off. "That's what God told me, Carl, and that's what I did!"

"Praise the Lord," I replied.

"Yes, indeed," he shot back. "Praise the Lord! He showed me the questions and then helped me with the answers! And his answers were much greater than mine could ever begin to be. Before, I thought the *abundant* life would be found when I got what I was striving for. The thing about it is, I was striving for the wrong thing!"

"I call heaven and earth to witness against you that today I have set before you life and death, blessing or curse. Oh, that you would choose life; that you and your children might live!" (Deut. 30:19).

An outstanding Christian woman stood before a throng in a huge auditorium and presented her testimony. I was among the listeners, and her words were embedded in my mind as she told of her search for a reason to be living: "Jesus Christ transformed my entire life, my reason for living, my purpose for life—well, just my everything!"

By seeking and following God's leadership, you can be transformed. Through Christ you can obtain the power to set and accomplish high quality ambitions that will bring forth the satisfaction and joy inherent within you. "For if a man is in Christ he becomes a new person altogether—the past is finished and gone, everything has become fresh and new" (2 Cor. 5:17, Phillips).

Are you in Christ and is he in you? This is the important question. Do you really know him in a personal way, day by day, or is it merely a passing acquaintance that is acknowledged every now and then? To gain real victory in your Christian life, you must go beyond the basic acknowledgement and perfunctory worship of Jesus. *Christianity is Christ in you and you in him.* It is when you seek, find, and follow his leadership in daily decisions that you begin to know him personally. When you and Christ are one—planning together, climbing together, attaining together—you can see the glow of victory on the horizon. "For it is God who is at work within you, giving you the will and the power to achieve his purpose" (Phil. 2:13, Phillips).

Looking at the "ambitious" warnings of Sallust, Shakespeare, and Burton, I concede that ambition, alone, is dangerous. However, forming high-quality, God-centered ambitions is the first step toward personal victory. It was this type of ambition T. D. English referred to when he said: "Ambition is the seed from which all growth of nobleness proceeds."

Quality ambition instilled by God was in the mind of Donald G. Mitchell when he asserted: "Ambition is the spur that makes man struggle with destiny. It is heaven's own incentive to make purpose great and achievement greater."

High-quality ambition can be yours if you go to God through prayer and Bible study; if you, in his presence, recognize your failures;

if you ask God, through his Son, to come into your life and live through you. High-quality ambition will be born and victory will come. "I stand silently before the Lord, waiting for him to rescue me" (Ps. 62:1).

You can do it!

4 / Believe!

"My God will supply all that you need from his glorious resources in Christ Jesus" (Phil. 4:19, Phillips).

Religion, psychology, and common sense all emphasize the importance of *belief.* An old Latin proverb says, "Believe that you have it, and you have it," meaning that belief is the motivating force which enables us to achieve our goals. It goes without saying that the goals for which we strive must be realistic. And they will be if we seek God's leadership in setting them.

Strong belief evokes the dominant best in one's nature. Jesus said, "*Anything* is possible if you have faith" (Mark 9:23). If we develop a great faith in God, we can develop a powerful belief in ourselves. This belief in ourselves will lead to a dynamic belief in the materializing of our ambitions. If we do not have a positive, hopeful, faith approach to our ambitions, we will never reach them.

"I am the Master of my Fate, I am the Captain of my Soul," is the way the poet Henley phrased it, and this places the initiative exactly where it should be—on our shoulders. Only *I* can believe in God through Christ, no one else can do it for me. Only *I* can believe in myself and my ambitions, no one else can intercede. Yes, God through his Son and through his Holy Spirit can direct and advise us, but we alone must do the believing.

There is nothing as important in our quest for real success as our mental attitudes toward ourselves. James Allen said, "A man is literally *what he thinks,* his character being the complete sum of all his thoughts." And, according to psychiatrist Karl Menninger, "Attitudes are more important than facts."

How true it is! How many times have you seen or heard of a "weaker" team defeating a "stronger" team? "On paper," the stronger team had everything going for them. They were *supposed* to win.

But they didn't because the weaker team was more *up* for the game. According to the cold facts, the weaker team didn't have a chance. But their positive, triumphant attitude erased all the cold facts. This is true in sports, business, politics, and life in general.

There is much more power behind our thoughts than most of us have ever realized. Many people say, "That 'power of positive thinking' junk is for the birds!" Other people say nothing at all because they have never even considered it. But the words, "For as he thinketh in his heart, so is he," are given deep meaning by Jesus' words: "If you had faith even as small as a tiny mustard seed you could say to this mountain, 'Move!' and it would go far away. Nothing would be impossible" (Matt. 17:20). Yet, people who accept other aspects of the Bible as fact refuse to accept this powerful promise from Jesus. And as they refuse, tiny molehills of resistance grow into mountains of opposition against dreams, hopes, and ideals.

When I was attending graduate school, my family and I went through a period of financial stress, a situation not uncommon to seminarians. Our budget was always tight, but one month in particular it appeared that there was no way possible for us to pay our bills and purchase food or anything else that required that green stuff we know as money. No way.

So I began to pray about it, with more intensity and more fervency than I had ever before experienced in my prayer life. To the effect, I prayed:

> Lord, you know what we need and you know what our creditors need. I'm going to seminary classes four hours a day, teaching school three hours, and serving as minister of youth in a church. I study and write in my "spare" time.
>
> Jean [my wife] is working too, God. But right now . . . well . . . you know the situation. And I pray, believing, that you are going to take what we're doing and use it in such a way that we're going to receive what we need.
>
> Thank you, Lord, for once again leading us through a difficult time and for helping us to grow stronger in faith as a result of it.

When I finished praying, I knew the solution to our problem was coming, and I told Jean it was, because that was one of the most meaningful prayers I had ever experienced. I had emptied myself of myself and turned the situation over to God, completely. I said: "God, I believe in you through Jesus, I believe in myself, and I believe in what I'm doing; and I know we're gonna' make it!"

Within a week's time, I received a check from a publisher for a play I had written and submitted several months earlier—the first payment I ever received for my Christian writing. Three days later, Jean got a raise in salary, a reward, according to her employer, for the fine work she was doing. We paid our bills, we ate . . . . Jesus said, "You can get anything—*anything* you ask for in prayer—if you believe" (Matt. 21:22).

Prayer and Belief Are Inseparable

Prayer and belief go together, for the acquiring of a dynamic, realistic faith is accomplished through prayer. If we accept the teachings of the Bible, we must grasp the truth that true, beseeching prayer is heard and answered.

But what is "true, beseeching prayer"? It is not something one reads from a book. It is not something a person memorizes and then repeats from habit. It is no superficial grouping of words tossed Godward with hopes that something might stick.

I know of no better definition of prayer than the statement I heard and wrote down. The source escapes me, but the idea didn't: "Prayer is the offering up of our desires unto God for things agreeable to His will." This places the focus where it belongs—on God and his will. But it also emphasizes that our desires are important.

True, beseeching prayer is when our souls reach out to God and we sincerely pour out our deep desires, realizing that above all, his will be done. If we pray this way, our prayers will be heard and answered as Jesus promised in John 14:14: "Yes, ask *anything*, using my name, and I will do it!"

You might say, "Carl, I definitely know of prayers that were not answered or even heard." Let me suggest that if your prayers seem to fall on deaf ears or get no answer, don't inspect the power of prayer and God. Inspect yourself.

Let me tell you of a man who prayed for wisdom and understanding but continued to read comic books, watch TV, and play golf in all his spare time. He made no attempt to experience any real communication with people, nor did he study, nor did he have time to know God better by delving into his Word. The man's situation was similar to that of the woman who prayed that she and her husband might be more compatible while she continued to belittle him, nag him, and attack any initiative he displayed.

Do you think the prayers of these two people were heard or answered? The point is this: "Faith that doesn't show itself by good works is no faith at all—it is dead and useless" (Jas. 2:17). Faith without works is dead. Prayer without works is never born!

Perhaps you might say, "Carl, I support my prayers with works, but still they are not heard or answered." If this is the case, I ask you if you have ever considered that your prayers may be foolish or unintelligent?

Our first words uttered to God in prayer should be, "Lord, teach us to pray." Often, we are guilty of seeking our base, uncultivated wills, rather than his. We are guilty of seeking to set our own goals and ambitions without consulting God. We go to him, saying, "I don't want advice, God—just results!" We can learn much from Jesus' plea: "My Father! If it is possible, let this cup be taken away from me. But I want your will, not mine" (Matt. 26:39).

Prayer must be an act of complete surrender and honesty as we relate to God.

I had several counseling sessions with a woman who is an alcoholic. She told me how she had prayed that God would help her stop drinking, but, in her words, "God paid me no mind." As we talked, I learned that, as is often the case, alcohol was not her problem. Frustrations, vague anxieties, general unhappiness—this was her problem. The alcohol was used as a poor replacement for the quality of life she had not obtained.

In the woman's life was hate, envy, jealousy, and bitterness toward people who appeared to have found the satisfaction she had never been able to grasp. I attempted to tactfully explain this to her, but she would not accept it. In so many words, she told me: "I want to keep my hate, envy, jealousy, and bitterness, but I want to get rid of the alcohol!" She was telling God, "We'll do it my way, or we won't do it at all!"

All too often, we go to God, telling him what we want, believing that we have the unalterable solution to a particular situation. We are afraid to open our "hidden" desires and failings to God. But, of course, he knows. And he knows that we know and that we're just playing a game. "Trust in the Lord with all thine heart; and lean not unto thine own understanding" (Prov. 3:5, KJV).

Trust in the Lord; believe in yourself. Prayer must be positive. Jesus emphasized this positive approach when he said: "You can get anything—*anything* you ask for in prayer—if you believe" (Matt. 21:22). We must have the feeling, the knowledge that our aspirations, forged and refined in the will of God, will be realized.

I am reminded of the story of the man who wanted to ease his financial burdens and relieve some of the difficulties of finding fresh vegetables at reasonable prices. He decided to plow up his back yard and plant a garden. The only problem was that there was a huge boulder in the middle of the yard. To get rid of the obstruction, he began to pray about it.

"Oh, God," he said with head bent low. "Oh, God, please remove the boulder from my yard so that I might plant a garden."

Then, he raised his head, opened his eyes, and looked out into the yard. The boulder was still there. "Huh!" the man said aloud to God. "I knew you couldn't do it!"

Anything you ask for in prayer *disbelieving*, forget it!

Jesus commanded that we ought to always pray and not fail in our prayer lives; the apostle Paul later phrased it, "Pray without ceasing" (1 Thess. 5:17, KJV). This means to pray about everything that merits an intelligent response.

I make it a habit to surround myself with *prayer reminders* so that I might truly attempt to pray without ceasing. Let me explain.

In my study, where I spend a large amount of my time in writing and preparing for engagements, I have posted the reminders. One such reminder is the sentence, "Those who can see the invisible can do the impossible." This typed sentence is on the top drawer of my file cabinet, and I see it each day as I sit at my desk. It reminds me to constantly visualize in my mind's eye the goals which, through God, I feel I am qualified to reach. It is important for us to have clear visions of our goals, and the more we look upon them the clearer they tend to become.

Another reminder is a wall poster which depicts a raccoon stretched out across a body of water, two paws clinging desperately to a boat and the other two paws tenaciously hanging onto a dock. Inscribed on the picture is, "Hang in there, baby!"

Looking at this particular poster, I put myself in the raccoon's place, knowing things sometimes get rough and it appears we won't make it. But the picture triggers the idea that God never calls on us to do anything we haven't the ability to do. Jesus tells us: "Because of your faith it will happen" (Matt. 9:29).

Some Bible verses adorn my walls and desk and serve as prayer reminders. I have framed the first check I received for writing to help me constantly recall the situation in which it was received. Attached to the bottom of the wastebasket next to my desk is a sticker which reads, "Smile—God Loves You." Into this can I have thrown reams of discarded paper used in an attempt to find the right words for a play or song or poem or book. The sticker always meets my eye when I empty the wastebasket and begin again.

The king in Shakespeare's *Hamlet* fails miserably in his attempt to pray. Of his failure he says:

"My words fly up, my thoughts remain below;
Words without thoughts never to heaven go."

Our prayers fail when they are words without thoughts. Our thoughts fail unless they are positive.

No Mind Is a Vacuum

We are constantly thinking. The mind cannot remain a vacuum.

It is either filled with creative, healthy, positive thoughts, with mediocre, wasted thoughts, or with damaging, defeating, negative thoughts. Therefore, it is vitally important that we train our thoughts upon quality things rather than fill our minds with "so-so" or, even worse, negative, debasing mental pictures.

A certain high school football coach was quite disturbed over the fact that his premier running back was performing way below his capability. After practice one day, all the boys had left the dressing room and the coach was walking through, on his way out also. He chanced to pass by the running back's locker and noticed the door was ajar. As he stepped over to close the door, he saw a large picture of a nude girl pasted on the inside of it. Smaller pictures of various parts of the female body were also posted on the door.

The coach stood alone in that locker room and realized why the running back was not realizing his potentialities. It was clear that the boy's mind was not on football, but was preoccupied with what was apparently an unhealthy, lustful view of sex. The last things the boy saw each day prior to going onto the field for a practice or a game were the pictures. They were the first things he saw upon his return from the field and the last things he saw before going home. They were the images which were being branded into his mind, day-in and day-out. The coach decided to change brands.

He chose not to say anything to the boy. Instead, he removed the pictures that day and replaced them with selections of his own. He cut a picture and caption from a magazine he had in his office. It was a dynamic picture of the Washington Redskins' coach, George Allen. The caption read: "No matter what the job, an ingredient of success is enthusiasm. Enthusiasm keeps you going."

The coach knew the boy was a professing Christian because they were members of the same church. So he placed a poster on the door which displayed these words:

> "What you are is God's gift to you—
> What you make of yourself is your gift to God."

The next day when the boy came to the locker room to get ready for practice, he swung open the door, saw the change which had taken place, and stood in silence as he read the words jumping out at him. Moisture crept into the eyes of this six-foot, two-inch, one hundred ninety-five pound running back. He sat on the bench by his locker and looked down at his feet. He said nothing to anyone about the switch. He knew the coach was behind it. He knew the coach cared about him as a football player and as a person. He knew he had been letting the coach down.

A transformed boy with a new perspective ran out onto the practice field that day, and he began running into the opponents' end zones in the games that followed. He began to grow as a football player and as a person.

Our minds develop in proportion to the manner in which they are fed. Emerson said, "A man is what he thinks about all day long." Marcus Aurelius said, "A man's life is what his thoughts make it." Norman Vincent Peale said, "Change your thoughts and you change your world." The Bible says, "For as he thinketh in his heart, so is he" (Prov. 23:7, KJV). It is claimed that a chain is no stronger than its weakest link. It may be that a person is no stronger than his weakest thought.

Nathaniel Hawthorne's story, "The Great Stone Face," illustrates that we become our thoughts. As the story goes, nature had carved the face into the side of a mountain. It was a strong, human face with wondrous features, but it also had the touch of the divine about it. Legend claimed that someday there would appear a person who would look like the Great Stone Face.

A boy named Ernest was enthralled by the face and he continually gazed upon it with admiration. Through all his childhood and even after he became a man, Ernest kept looking at the great face and also for the person who would be like it. Then one day, as the people of the surrounding countryside were discussing the legend, Ernest's face assumed a grandeur of expression as he set his mind upon an idea he wanted to share. Suddenly, someone cried out, "Behold! Behold! Ernest is himself the likeness of the Great Stone Face!" Everyone turned to see. True enough, he was. *Ernest had become like his thoughts.*

"Fix your thoughts on what is true and good and right. Think about things that are pure and lovely, and dwell on the fine, good things in others. Think about all you can praise God for and be glad about" (Phil. 4:8).

Walt Whitman, the great American poet, wrote that he found himself and discovered and developed his potentialities through strong belief and resultant enthusiasm. He said, "I was simmering, really simmering; Emerson brought me to a boil." So many people today are simmering. But most of these people will "simmer" their lives away, never ever coming to a boil. Even though success appears to be "just around the corner," they continue to live on in frustrated ineffectiveness.

When do you propose to do the wonderful things you have been dreaming about, to live the life-style you have been intending to live? Are you waiting for "the right time"? The time is now. Are you waiting for "luck"? Through the leadership of God, it is up to you to make your own "luck."

Nothing is more demoralizing than to be constantly wishing and wanting and dreaming of the great things we are going to do or the happiness we are going to experience or the joy and peace we're going to find—and then not making the needed effort to accomplish our goals.

If a poem is never heard, what good is it? If a book is never read, what good is it? If a song is never sung, what good is it?

An architect can draw beautiful plans, but these plans are worthless unless he puts them to use. "I'm going to build this house one of these days," the architect said in 1963. "This is the house I intend to build," the architect said in 1973. "These are the plans for the house I was going to build," the architect said in 1983.

We should all take time to ask ourselves if we are constantly thinking upon our "life theme." Are we making the most of our opportunities? God is interested in our total lives. He wants us to believe in him and believe in ourselves. He wants us to be happy, healthy, prosperous, victorious—not frustrated shells of empty people. "How we thank you, Lord! Your mighty miracles give proof that you care" (Ps. 75:1).

God is calling *you* to believe in him, to believe in yourself, to believe in your ambition. Fail to heed this call to belief and it will one day grow so faint it cannot be heard at all. To you, God will be dead, you will be dead, and your ambitions will be scattered among the ashes.

It is impossible for an unbeliever to be victorious. But yet, it is just as impossible for a real believer to fail. Keep the right ideals and objectives constantly before you, and your chances of succeeding will be tremendously multiplied. Through God's leadership and through wise human counsel, determine what your true talents are. Dedicate these talents to a worthwhile cause, remembering that they are a gift from God and not to be taken lightly or without due responsibility. Thinking such as this will lead you on to real victory.

How great it is to be stuck with hope (as the song from *South Pacific* suggests), with belief, and with the enthusiasm needed to carry you on to victory.

You can do it!

5/Plan, Pursue, and Persevere

A *success* is one who decided to succeed and did something about it. A *failure* is one who decided to succeed and did nothing.

After you discover that only through seeking and following God's will can one find true personal victory, you must then do something about it. By continuing to adhere to God's leadership, you must formulate a definite purpose toward which to work and you must devise a definite plan for attaining that purpose. Next, you must put your actions where your mind is.

Five men intended to take trips. The first man didn't know where he was going, so he just packed his suitcase, got into his car, and started driving. He hoped he might eventually arrive at his destination and thus discover what his destination was.

The second man knew his destination, but he didn't take the time to sit down with a map to determine how to get there. So, he packed his suitcase, got into his car, and started driving, hoping he would eventually happen upon the place for which he was looking.

The third man knew his destination also. He obtained a map and inspected it closely. After carefully planning the route he should take, he packed his suitcase, got into his car, but then lacked the initiative to make the trip.

The fourth man also knew his destination and he acquired a map with which to plan his trip. After determining the route he would take, he packed his suitcase, got into his car, and started on the journey. However, the man soon became tired and discouraged, so he stopped his car and decided to go no further.

The fifth man, as did the previous three, knew his destination. And, like the two men before him, he obtained the latest map, inspected it closely, and carefully planned the best possible route. Then, he packed his suitcase, got into his car, and started on the journey. The way was sometimes rough; he, at times, grew tired and discouraged. However, he was determined to reach his destination, and he did.

Many people "don't get anywhere" in life because they don't know where they want to go. Other people know where they want to go, but they don't construct plans and methods on how to get there. Others know where they want to go and know how to get there, but they lack the incentive or enthusiasm to embark on the trip. Still others know where they want to go and know how to get there; they begin on the trip but give up along the way. Finally, however, some people know where they are going and how to get there, and they go—all the way.

This fifth group of people has realized the importance of the words of the historian Arnold Toynbee when he described a method by which to defeat apathetic mediocrity and find success: "Apathy can only be overcome by enthusiasm, and enthusiasm can only be aroused by two things; first an ideal which takes the imagination by a storm, and second, a definite intelligible plan for carrying that ideal into practice."

In order to succeed, you must clearly visualize your ambition and concentrate on this vision. You must "map your way" to reach the ambition and then work to follow the route and arrive at your destination.

When writing to inspire the first-century Christians at Corinth, the apostle Paul compared growing in Christ and reaching goals to a race.

> "In a race everyone runs but only one person gets first prize. So run your race to win.
>
> To win the contest you must deny yourselves many things that would keep you from doing your best. An athlete goes to all this trouble just to win a blue ribbon or a silver cup, but we do it for a heavenly reward that never disappears.
>
> So I run straight to the goal with purpose in every step. I fight to win. I'm not just shadow-boxing or playing around.
>
> Like an athlete I punish my body, treating it roughly, training

it to do what it should, not what it wants to. Otherwise I fear that after enlisting others for the race, I myself might be declared unfit and ordered to stand aside" (1 Cor. 9:24-27).

Win is the name of the game. Yet, we are living in a mediocre society, comprised of mediocre people, because of the lack of a definite purpose, plan, and pursuit in the lives of so many individuals. It is good to dream, but too many people utilize dreams only as escapes from reality, never uniting them with reality. Rather than having a purpose, plan, and adequate pursuit, entire lives are rationalized away in daydreams.

Longfellow said: "We judge ourselves by what we feel capable of doing, while others judge us by what we have already done." It is the person one thinks he is, compared to the person he actually is at the present time. Frustrations are born and reared when one continues to see himself as what he could be but never becomes. His unrealistic dreamworld begins to choke him.

I talked with a man who, at the age of forty-eight, was suffering greatly as a result of finally seeing himself as he really was and comparing what he saw to what he thought he was. For years, he had been living in a world of fantasy, always seeing himself as successful and happy, but never being so, and never actively planning for and pursuing his goal as he should and could. The man's dreamworld was shattered when his financial difficulties reached an all-time high. His wife left him and took their children when she could bear no more of his dreaming and the resultant problems the dreaming had brought upon the family.

I encountered this man at a conference I was leading. When he spoke with me, for the first time he admitted to himself that his goals for success and happiness had never been attained and probably never would be. Even though he had caused his family to suffer for years and had himself become a victim of the "ups and downs" of manic-depressive moods, only now did he "wake up" and see himself as a *failure* as a husband and father. Only now did he see himself as a *disappointment* to himself.

Initially, the man would not accept the blame for his failure and disappointment. He would not accept the idea that the fault lay within himself. He looked for scapegoats on which to shove the blame. Eventually, however, he did accept the blame. Now, through the leadership of God, he is realistically trying to pick up the pieces of his life and make it really count. Success and happiness may still be on his horizon.

It is frustrating for a young adult to continually think about what he or she is going to do, while never doing it. Many people think about having high-quality attitudes, life-styles, priorities, and careers, but somehow never get around to carrying through with the thoughts. The frustrations grow into dangerous life-draining depression as the young adult advances into an anxiety-laden middle age. Then, there comes an ever-increasing awareness that life is rapidly passing. Friends die; children grow up and leave home; dreams evaporate among goals that never materialized. But it doesn't have to be this way.

In an attempt to overcome the pitfalls of apathetic mediocrity and to conquer the trap of "always meaning to, but never doing," we can respond positively to the advice presented by the apostle Paul:

> "As Christ's soldier do not let yourself become tied up in worldly affairs, for then you cannot satisfy the one who has enlisted you in his army.
>
> Follow the Lord's rules for doing his work, just as an athlete either follows the rules or is disqualified and wins no prize.
>
> Work hard, like a farmer who gets paid well if he raises a large crop.
>
> Think over these three illustrations, and may the Lord help you to understand how they apply to you" (2 Tim. 2:4-7).

As suggested by Paul, we must *want* to win; we must know and abide by the guidelines and rules for winning; and we must exercise discipline and denial in our lives to accomplish our victory. If we want to become what we have the potential to become, we've got to "get it all together." In order to succeed, the total person has to be involved. Our mental, physical, and spiritual lives must be one with God.

Winning, As a Way of Life

A few years ago it was my privilege to attend a banquet at which NFL quarterback Fran Tarkenton was the featured speaker. The football season was over and a quarterback club was staging its annual evening of fun and celebration. Laughter and light talk were prevalent in the hotel banquet room as a large gathering listened to the emcee's humorous stories and tackled plates stacked high with food.

Then, it came time for the introduction of the special guest speaker. Fran Tarkenton received a thunderous round of applause as he stepped to the podium. Beginning with a couple of funny stories and a big smile which stretched from ear to ear, Fran kept alive the frivolous mood of the gala affair.

Soon, however, Tarkenton, former All-American at the University of Georgia and veteran leader of the Minnesota Vikings, began to insert a serious note into his address.

"You don't always see it on your TV screens, but I've been out there and watched those two hundred eighty-five pound linemen belt each other around," the minister's son said. "They go through the pain and agony just for a hope. The hope of victory."

He paused and seemed to look into the eyes of every individual in the room. "I've never been associated with anything quite like it," the scrambling quarterback added. "They're out there playing for the glory of the team and not for the glory of the individual."

By this time, Fran's audience was becoming spellbound. He went on to tell of the importance of having a desire to win—not only in sports, but in life itself. After clearly defining the difference between a *good sport* and a *good loser,* this leader in the Fellowship of Christian Athletes stated, "Show me a good loser, and I'll show you a loser! Losing should always make us more ready to meet the challenge, and some day we'll have victory."

No one in the room was sipping tea or coffee now. No one chewed or sucked on a piece of ice. Fran Tarkenton continued.

"I'll never forget that first game I played with the Minnesota

Vikings. We were an expansion team and we were not given a chance to win. We were in the locker room getting ready to play the oldest team in professional football—the Chicago Bears.

"I was a twenty-one-year-old rookie and thirty-nine men were looking to me for leadership. Believe me, I was scared and nervous. I went over my 'ready list' again, trying to remember what I was supposed to do in certain situations. We were twenty-one point underdogs and there was a full house on hand to watch the Vikings play their first pro game.

"We beat the Bears, 37-13, and I'll never forget the feeling I had. I was on top of the world. I was anxious to meet the reporters, because I had thrown four touchdown passes and had run for another. I stayed for about an hour after the game talking to the writers. Then I went into the dressing room and took a long shower.

"When I came out of the dressing room, I didn't leave the stadium immediately. I went back down the tunnel and onto the field. I wanted to recapture the victory we had won. But, instead of fifty thousand people, there were fifty thousand empty seats. The wind was blowing and it was cold.

"That taught me one of the greatest lessons I have ever learned in life. I knew that I could never recapture that victory. I knew I had to press on to greater victories and greater achievements. That's how it should be."

A standing ovation accompanied Fran Tarkenton as he walked away from the podium. Words of wisdom accompanied the crowd who walked away from the hotel banquet room later that evening.

Winning is a way of life.

Simply put, if we want to realize our potential, if we want to become what we can become, if we want to gain the joy and satisfaction that can be ours, we have to give life our best. A winner constantly thinks upon his "life theme." Other aspects of life are built around his primary purpose or goal or ambition. Daily, he is actively working toward that goal.

Mahatma Gandhi, the great leader of India, said: "Only give up a thing when you want some other condition so much that the thing has no longer any attraction for you, or when it seems to interfere with that which is more greatly desired."

In setting, planning for, and striving for your goal, be on the lookout for side issues which might detract from your primary purpose. Get rid of superfluous diversions which may be fleetingly pleasant but not lastingly worthwhile. It has been said that success in life is a process of selection and elimination. That is, to have sufficient time for things that count, you must cut out things that do not count. This, of course, is what Paul was emphasizing when he wrote: "All these things that I once thought very worthwhile—now I've thrown them all away so that I can put my trust and hope in Christ alone" (Phil. 3:7).

Take Nothing for Granted

"Keep me from deliberate wrongs; help me to stop doing them. Only then can I be free of guilt and innocent of some great crime" (Ps. 19:13).

We are walking on dangerous ground when we "just assume" our dreams will materialize without our working to make it so. The psalmist realized that such presumption could lead to one's eventual downfall, and no one is exempt from such a danger.

In a city where I lived several years ago, there was a boy in junior high who caught the imagination of the city's football coaches and fans alike. Many predicted the boy would make the all-conference and all-state teams when he joined the high school ranks. As a junior-high player, this boy set all records pertaining to yards rushed for and to points scored. With these records in mind, there were even predictions the running back would be an all-American in college and then an all-pro.

His first year in high school, however, the boy did not even make first string. No doubt, he had the inherent potential. But he got to the point where he "just assumed" he was going to be great. The discipline, dedication, and self-denial that he had utilized to develop into an outstanding junior-high player were forgotten. He became careless; he began to take things for granted. A loss of speed and strength, a lack of sufficient determination, and an entrance of a negative attitude became evident. Because of *presumption,* he never reached his potential.

At the close of a worship service, I carefully observed several young people as they publicly responded to an invitation. Six of them came forward to share with the pastor their desires to *rededicate* themselves to the Lord. This is a great decision for Christians to make. But one girl who came forward had made five such commitments during the past two years. One boy was now expressing rededication number four. The other youths had also taken similar walks during the past couple of years.

Following the service that evening, I asked the young people who had made the decisions to come to my office to talk with me. "How do you feel when you believe God is leading you to rededicate your Christian lives?" I asked them. They all answered in essentially the same way.

"I feel I have got away from God," one of them said. "But during the service, I was drawn back close to him again. I don't know—the prayers, the songs, the reading of the Bible, the sermon—everything seemed to make me feel I was right next to God and that he was right next to me. And I wanted it to stay that way."

I then asked them what had happened in the past when they had rededicated their lives.

"Things were good for awhile," one girl responded and the others agreed, "but after a time, I seemed to fall back to where I was to start with. I seemed to drift away from God."

"What exactly did you do when you rededicated your lives the other times?"

"What do you mean?" one of the group replied.

"I mean, well . . . for one thing, did you have a big change in your prayer lives?"

"No, not really," was the group response.

"Well," I continued, "did you find yourselves spending a lot more time in personal Bible study?"

"No, not really," was the group answer.

"What about an increase in your Christian witnessing or in your church involvement?" I asked next. "Did you see a change?"

"No, not really," was the group response.

I paused and looked at the young people and then shared with them what I had been suspecting all along. "In the past, you have not rededicated your lives to God," I told them, "but you can really do it this time." They were surprised at my words, but they understood me when I told them that they had experienced the working of the Holy Spirit in the worship services. They had felt a closeness to God, and in essence had asked God to keep them close.

I went on to explain: "What you said to God is, 'Lord, I like feeling close to you and I want you to keep me here. I'm not going to take time to study the Bible or spend more time in prayer or talk with others about you, but I want you to keep me feeling good.' " They understood.

We must understand. To presume on God and on success leads to defeat. God has endowed us with abilities and opportunities. Utilizing these gifts wisely and diligently, we may taste victory.

Do It Now

> "He (Jesus) invited a man to come with him and to be his disciple, the man agreed—but wanted to wait until his father's death.
>
> Jesus replied, 'Let those without eternal life concern themselves with things like that. Your duty is to come and preach the coming of the Kingdom of God to all the world.'
>
> Another said, 'Yes, Lord, I will come, but first let me ask permission of those at home.'
>
> But Jesus told him, 'Anyone who lets himself be distracted from the work I plan for him is not fit for the Kingdom of God" (Luke 9:59-62).

The man who told Jesus he wanted to "wait until his father's death," was apparently suggesting that he postpone following Jesus until his father died so that he might receive an inheritance and thus have some security. The father may have died within a week or a month or a year or ten years. Responding to the man's request, Jesus essentially said, "Follow me now, or forget it!"

The greatest labor-saving device ever invented is "tomorrow." However, as I heard one speaker so aptly phrase it: "The verdant green meadows of tomorrow can turn today into a barren desert. He who has a taste only for anticipations will be undernourished. The real meat-and-potatoes joy in life is the here and now."

The here and now! That's where things are happening. But, oh the number of people who live for tomorrow—always delaying, putting off—constantly wishing and waiting but never doing.

A girl standing five feet, four inches tall and weighing one hundred forty-five pounds decided she was going to diet and lose some of her excess baggage. She made up her mind to begin the diet bright and early the next morning—because, after all, the dawning of a new day is the best time to get started on anything. She went to bed. Morning came.

As the girl awoke, she smelled the tempting fragrance of bacon and eggs and fresh biscuits and other delicacies that her mother very seldom prepared. "I'll begin the diet at noon," the girl told herself as she delved into the breakfast.

Lunchtime arrived—and would you believe it? Usually, the school cafeteria offered absolutely nothing appealing to the girl. On this particular day, however, it featured a meal that undeniably pleased her palate. "Oh, well," she explained to herself, "it's always best to begin a diet at home, anyway, so I'll get it underway tonight."

You'll never guess what happened. That evening, her mother prepared the girl's favorite dish, and, of course, it was irresistible. "Tomorrow," she rationalized to herself, "I will begin the diet." However, as the old saying goes, *Tomorrow never comes.* For this reason, the anonymous writer of an ancient Sanskrit poem admonishes:

> Look to this day
> for it is life
> the very life of life
> In its brief course lie all

the realities and truths of existence
the joy of growth
the splendor of action
the glory of power
For yesterday is but a memory
And tomorrow is only a vision
But today well lived
makes every yesterday a memory of happiness
and every tomorrow a vision of hope
Look well, therefore, to this day!

Many of today's failing, frustrated, unhappy people see themselves as successful and happy tomorrow, but tomorrow they will be the same as today, because they are not doing anything about their situations *now*. Numerous "overnight successes" spent years and years in the *now* to reach their goals. Often, when we look upon someone who is happily successful in the best sense of the word, we tend to overlook the time he was involved in "climbing the stairs." But, because he invested dedication, discipline, and work in yesterday, he is reaping the benefits *now*.

I cannot play a piano. In 1965, I felt a desire to learn how to play, so I took some lessons. After only a short while, however, I gave up the idea, apparently because my desire was not strong enough. Had I continued with the lessons and had I continued practicing, studying, and playing, today I would probably be able to do quite well. But I can't play.

I do not believe that not being able to play the piano will cause me to be unhappy and unsuccessful. However, there are things I can think of, had I left them undone in the past, that would contribute to my downfall in the *now*.

The question arises: What are some things you should be doing now, but aren't doing? Tomorrow, will you pay dearly for the lack of dedication, discipline, and work that is evident in your life today?

Six years ago, in a conference in which I was speaking, I met a young lady who told me she wanted to be a writer. At her request, I spent some time with her, anwering some questions she had and offering some tips which had helped me in my writing and in getting my writing published. When that young lady left the conference room that day, I told my wife that the potential writer seemed to "have a lot on the ball" and that she would more than likely be doing some good things.

A few months ago at another conference, this potential writer walked up to where I stood and said, "Remember me?" At first, I didn't. But when she reminded me of our talk six years ago, I remembered.

She smiled a big smile and told me she had read some of my recent writings and had seen a couple of my latest dramas. I, of course, was pleased. Then, I asked her, "How is your writing coming along? What have you had published?"

"Pretty good," she responded to my first question. "Nothing, yet," was her reply to question number two.

She went on to explain that in the past six years she had written a few poems, but had not submitted them to a magazine or publisher. She said she had some songs, but had not written them down yet or put them on tape. "I've started a couple of dramas," she told me, "and I'm working on some short stories and I've got a good idea for a book that I'm going to write one of these days."

Tomorrow: the greatest labor-saving device ever invented.

Tomorrow: I will get serious about Christianity. I will set, plan, and work for high-quality goals. I will really begin to live rather than merely exist. "How do you know what will happen tomorrow?" (Jas. 4:14, Phillips). "Now is the acceptable time" (2 Cor. 6:2, Phillips).

Do it now!

Keep on Keeping On

When *Mr. Failure* grabs me by my right arm and *Mr. Discouragement* takes hold of my left, each pulling and twisting with all their strength, I like to think about a man who struggled against these two foes most of his life. As a youngster, things were extremely difficult for him and as a young man his first venture into the business world met with dismal failure.

The year following his business failure, he became extremely interested in politics, ran for the state legislature, and was defeated soundly. The next year, he entered into another business enterprise and again tasted defeat. Three years later, with things going from bad to worse, he suffered a nervous breakdown which was heavily veiled with discouragement. But the man rested, talked with the Lord and with himself, and got his bearings.

Feeling back on top of things, he ran for a top political office two years after the nervous breakdown and was defeated. Two years later, he took another bite of bitter political defeat. Down, but not out, he courageously ran for Congress three years later, but again met *Mr. Failure* face-to-face. *Mr. Discouragement* spent some time with the man, but the man reorganized his determined efforts and ran a concentrated race for Congress five years later. He lost.

He licked his wounds and planned for the future. Seven years after his Congressional defeat, he tossed his political hat into the ring for a seat in the Senate. He lost, just as he did the following year when, with high hopes, he ran for vice-president of the United States. Political defeat number eight came two years later when he again sought a Senate seat.

Needless to say, things looked bleak for this man who was widely known as an habitual loser. Nevertheless, still unwilling to sit down and coddle *Mr. Defeat* in his lap and let *Mr. Discouragement* get a firm grasp of his very heart and soul, the man continued to talk with the Lord and with himself and with knowledgeable advisors. Two years following his last political setback, the man shot for the highest elected office in the land. He won, and became President of the United States in 1860. Abraham Lincoln kept on keeping on.

The lack of persistence is one of the major causes of failure. At the same time, history has testified to the fact that the lack of persistence is a weakness common to the majority of people. There is an endless list registering the names of people who attempted to achieve something and then gave up in disappointment at their initial failure. Another list of equal size names those people who never even attempted to achieve what they wanted because they were afraid they might fail.

In order to be successful, you must recognize the difference between *temporary defeat* and *total defeat.* With the right attitude and the proper amount of persistence, temporary defeat can spur you on to greater heights as a person, a Christian, and the master of a life-style which will afford you true success. In our society it is a common habit for one to quit when he experiences what should be viewed as merely temporary defeat. But when he quits, it becomes total defeat.

As a college student, I was assigned to read *Lust for Life,* the biographical novel about Vincent Van Gogh by Irving Stone. At first, the reading was nothing more than an assignment. Soon, it became a fascinating experience. The literature professor had allowed us a month in which to read the book—I absorbed it in three days. I was captivated by Van Gogh's life and awed by the manner in which Stone had written about it.

Later, I was shocked when I learned that *Lust for Life* had been rejected by seventeen publishers before it was finally accepted for publication! Seventeen publishers told Irving Stone, now the acknowledged master of the biographical novel, that his writing was not good enough to be published. *Lust for Life* became a best-seller, and since that time Stone has had at least fifteen other books that have made the best-seller lists.

As a beginning writer, I was amazed, but encouraged, at the number of best-selling books that were originally "rejects." Comparatively speaking, there aren't too many books around which weren't rejected by one or more publishers prior to eventually getting into print. Some of the number one best-sellers of the past few years received pink slips of rejection during their infancy.

At times the rejecting publishers encouraged the authors to continue their work, just as we sometimes receive encouragement from others when we experience temporary defeat in our lives. God is our main source of encouragement if we are abiding in his will which glorifies Christ and leads us on to personal victory. "If God is on our side, who can ever be against us?" (Rom. 8:31).

An important survey which has been circulating in the business world for the past few years indicates that approximately one half of all professional salesmen give up after receiving one no from a prospective customer. Another one fifth make two calls before giving up, and about one tenth make three or four calls before quitting. The remaining twenty percent of the salesmen make at least five calls on their prospects. These twenty percent make approximately eighty percent of all sales. That is why, financially speaking, some of the most unsuccessful people in the world are salesmen and some of the most successful people in the world are salesmen.

A person with perseverance succeeds. A person with perseverance sets high-quality goals, plans for reaching them, works for their attainment, and eventually achieves his God-led ambition. A person with perseverance knows what true joy is all about. A person with perseverance defeats defeat and tastes the sweetness that only victory can bring.

You can do it!

6/Watch Out For Ruts!

Far away there in the sunshine
are my highest aspirations.
I may not reach them, but I
can
look
up
and see their beauty,
believe in them,
and try to follow where they
lead.

As an epilogue to the above lines by Louisa May Alcott, I add: *Watch out for ruts! Ruts* stand between people and goals. *Ruts* are great, natural enemies to ambition. *Ruts* lead to total failure.

As a young boy growing up in a small town, I had the freedom to ride my bicycle throughout our community. One weekly excursion I always enjoyed was my trip to the local movie theater on Friday night. I can now readily recall one such Friday in particular.

I left home earlier than usual that evening and arrived at the theater before the box office had even opened. Another boy on a bicycle had arrived early also; he was older than I and a somewhat distant friend.

"Wanna play follow-the-leader?" he asked me as we sat on our bikes in front of the still-closed theater and looked at the billboards and pictures advertising the upcoming movie.

In response, I sort of shrugged my shoulders, more interested in the movie I was going to see than in the game he suggested.

"Come on," he coaxed, "It'll be thirty minutes before the show starts."

"OK," I said. We began the game. Since the other boy was older, he, of course, was the self-chosen leader.

We rode down Main Street, which didn't take long, and swerved around some fire hydrants and parking meters and "jumped" a few lingering water puddles. At the far end of Main, we turned right at the city hall and pedaled toward a part of town known as "The Crossing." Adventurously riding up and down a few steep banks, we made a sharp left turn at the intersection of Twelfth and Maple, coming dangerously close to a couple of cars parked near the curb. The paved street soon became a gravel street which narrowed to become a wooden bridge over a large ditch. The "leader" fearlessly neared the bridge. It wasn't very wide and had no protective side railings. There were grooves or ruts in its base because the planks did not meet.

The older boy stood upright on his bicycle pedals and pumped them vigorously. He sped quickly across the rickety bridge with ease. Safely on the other side, he dramatically applied his brakes and noisily slung gravel as he spun around and smiled at my hesitation to follow. I was stopped at the edge of the bridge, looking down at the concrete culvert which lay imposingly fifteen feet below.

"Come on!" he prodded. His voice was edged with impatient sarcasm.

I looked up at him, glanced back down at the concrete, then turned my attention to the bridge itself.

"What are you—chicken or something?" he continued to taunt me.

I bit my bottom lip and pushed down on the left pedal. The right pedal rotated around, and I was on my way across. But I was going too slowly and the bicycle began to wobble. The front wheel slipped off the large middle plank on which I had started my trek. The wheel then lodged in one of the ruts between the planks; the bicycle and I suddenly became motionless. The stillness was soon disrupted, however, and the last thing I remember as the bicycle tilted sideways is that the concrete seemed to rush up to meet me.

I awoke in my bedroom later that evening and saw my parents

and our family doctor standing over me. The doctor smiled, shook his head, and said softly, "You're a lucky boy—a mighty lucky boy." "Luck" doesn't always accompany ruts.

Without permanent damage (only a slight concussion, a terrible headache, and a missed movie) I escaped the rut in which the bicycle tire became stuck. Since that time, I have been in and out of other ruts as I have been in and out of God's will and leadership. Some of these ruts have injured me and delayed me in reaching quality goals. Some have taught me great lessons. All of them have accentuated the fact that every worthy achievement is accomplished not by personal might or power, but only *by the Spirit of the Lord.*

As a child, teenager, and adult, each of us encounters ruts that can lead to temporary defeat or possibly total defeat. Therefore, just as there are signs along our highways to warn us of approaching dangers so that we may avoid them, I would like to erect some warning signs in this chapter.

Some of you may have already confronted some of the ruts I want to warn against; some of you may be bogged down in one or more of the ruts right now. Others of you may be unsuspectingly approaching the ruts which lie just around the corner.

Choose Associates Wisely

No matter in what vocation or life-style you may be involved, be extremely careful when choosing the people with whom you come in frequent contact. We have heard the adage, "We are known by the company we keep," and this wise saying is so true. Numerous people have met with total failure in life because they have chosen their companions unwisely. Humans have a tendency to absorb attitudes, actions, and reactions from one another, many times without even realizing they are doing so. Beliefs, goals, ideals, and ambitions are passed from one person to another. Strengths and weaknesses flow from one companion to another as if by osmosis.

I would never have gotten in that rut on the bridge if the older boy had not talked me into it. I didn't really want to play "follow the leader" that Friday evening. And I certainly didn't have any desire to cross that wobbly bunch of planks known as a bridge. But I did. The boy influenced me to do so, and I did it.

I talked with a concerned parent not long ago who told me of her daughter's dilemma. The girl had just entered the ninth grade and was caught between pleasing herself and her family or pleasing her friends. The girl had always made *A*'s and *B*'s in school without any difficulty. Now, however, she found if she achieved grades higher than a *C*, she was ridiculed by the other kids in her class and called a "wiseacre" or "goody-goody" or "genius." The girl was capable of *A*'s and *B*'s, but the group she had chosen as "friends" put her down if she did so.

Another mother came to a counseling session scared sick. Her daughter had told her that she had not yet been involved with drugs, alcohol, or sexual intercourse, but, in the words of the mother, "She told me she didn't know how much longer she could hold off. She said the other kids thought she was a weirdo or something."

One of the greatest gifts one person can give another is the motivation to surround oneself with positive people. No matter where you are in life at this particular moment or where you intend to go, it will make all the difference in the world if you associate with people who are striving for high-quality ambitions. We gradually become what we are by a process of identification with others.

That is why it is extremely important to keep God as your constant companion and to "pray without ceasing." But we must never overlook the element of human association. We must go to all lengths to keep in an atmosphere that arouses high-quality goals. We should purposely seek out people who will positively stimulate us to greater heights. One of the greatest mistakes one can make is to leave the structuring of his environment and the grouping of his friends to *chance.*

A sixteen-year-old boy accepted Christ as his Savior and pledged to let him be Lord of his life. This boy had been associating with a group of kids who exhibited anti-Christian thoughts and behaviors. He liked these kids and wanted to share Christ with them. When he continued his association with them, however, he quickly discovered that they were stronger non-Christians than he was a Christian. He soon found that they were pulling him back to where he used to be, rather than his pulling them to where he presently was. "What should I do?" he asked me in desperation.

"Pull away from them," I replied. "Pull away until you've had a chance to grow and mature in Christ. After you gain strength through prayer and Bible study and Christian fellowship, then you will be prepared to lead others." I then got my Bible and turned to 2 Timothy 2:22, to share with him this same advice from Paul: "Run from anything that gives you the evil thoughts that young men often have, but stay close to anything that makes you want to do right. Have faith and love, and enjoy the companionship of those who love the Lord and have pure hearts."

I confess that my immediate family of friends is small, even though I am associated with many people on a less intimate basis. The same is true for my wife, Jean, and we are leading our son, Carl "Two," to also be selective. This, of course, does not mean to be snobbish or stuck-up, but it does mean to avoid the negative influence of other people.

Will Rogers said that he never met a person he didn't like. This is saying a lot and is evidence of an admirable trait that is worthy of everyone's attention. But I am sure that Will Rogers was very much aware that one of our most common weaknesses is the habit of leaving our minds open to negative influences. We can strive to "like" everyone and, as Christ teaches, to "love" everyone—but this does not mean we should not guard against associating with people who will do us more harm than good.

I want my daily associates to be people who, to some degree, understand me—my philosophies, my beliefs, my goals, and my ambitions. I want my "friends" to be people who believe in me and in what I'm doing. I want to surround myself with companions who encourage me to make the most of my life, and I want to do the same for them.

This is not to say that I want positive, optimistic, high-quality goal seekers around me for purely selfish reasons. At the same time they are sharing with me, I want to share with them. I want to influence them as they give of themselves and "rub off" on me. Then it will be a case of people helping people, and this is the thrust of Christianity. "So we, being many, are one body in Christ, and every one members one of another" (Rom. 12:5, KJV).

Only yesterday I talked with a friend who is growing and maturing in Christ. She told me of meeting another woman for the first time and of the immediate bond which sprang up between the two of them. "As soon as I was introduced to her I knew that she knew the Lord," my friend shared with me, "and I felt as if the two of us had always known one another." As we continued to discuss the new but promising relationship, my friend said, "I want to be around this woman a lot—to talk with her and to experience things together in Christ."

If only more marriages had such a basic, supportive love, the "romantic" love would not wear so thin. So many times, marriage partners are "bad" for one another and cause one another great harm. There are numerous miserable marriages in which the so-called *partners* are not "partners" at all, but enemies who daily destroy goals and ambitions and all possibilities for success.

We must choose vocational associates wisely, exhibit caution and concern in forming friendships, and, by all means, make sure that our marriage partners are truly *partners*. Our selections in these vital areas can make all the difference in the world between our succeeding or failing in life, between our being happy or miserable, between our being fulfilled or frustrated.

Don't Live in Past Failures

"A Loser's Motto"

I don't have time for now.
I am too busy reflecting
upon my sad past,
my mistakes
and failures,
thinking of the

anxiety-laden
future
they
will
cause.

A sixteen-year-old girl entered my office one day, sat down at my invitation, and then suddenly blurted, "I had sex last Friday night." She went on to tell me that she "really didn't care all that much for the guy," but that she and her regular boy friend had a big squabble and the Friday night date sort of caught her on the rebound. She continued pouring out herself to me, saying that this was the first time she had engaged in sexual intercourse and that she felt "dirty and trashy."

I let the girl talk as much as she wanted to and then I supported her idea that she had, indeed, done something wrong. But I went on to tell her that her life was not "ruined" as she claimed it now was. I told her that we all make mistakes, that we all are guilty of turning our backs on God and then acting without considering what he would have us to do.

"But I'll never be the same again," she told me, tears flooding her eyes.

"You're right," I replied. "You'll never be the same." I paused and looked at her as she stared wide-eyed at me. Then, I continued. "As a result of what happened, you'll become much weaker as a person and a Christian—or—much stronger."

"What do you mean?" she asked, getting caught up in what I had said, using a finger to dry her eyes.

"This is a crisis in your life," I told her, "and I don't want to say, 'Aw, it's nothing, just forget it.' But the way you react to the crisis is much more important than the crisis itself."

As we continued to talk, I got my Bible and turned to John 8:1-11, and shared with the girl the account of the woman caught in adultery. "Jesus is the same today," I said, "and if you go to him, asking for forgiveness and strength, he will forgive you and supply you with a peace of mind you wouldn't believe possible." " 'Neither do

I condemn you,' said Jesus to her. 'Go away now and do not sin again'" (John 8:11, Phillips).

When this sixteen-year-old girl had entered my office, she was distraught and felt that "she just had to talk with somebody." She was in danger of letting a past failure discolor her present and distort her future. But through the leadership of Christ and through the experience of struggling with personal past failures, I was able to assist her in developing an attitude in which she sought forgiveness without lingering in the dark shadows of failure.

I truly believe that God desires us only to dwell on failures long enough to let it be known to him that we are sorry for what we have done and that we ask his forgiveness. This is not to say that we should repress our failures. For when we do this, they become cancers which eat away at our present and future and give Satan a foothold to suggest that we live with dark secrets that cannot be shared even with God himself.

As I told the sixteen-year-old girl that day, the ultimate objective in life is to know and obey God's will. This knowledge and obedience can never take place unless we are honest with God and with ourselves. "This can be a great, positive turning point in your life," I told the girl. "Put your trust in God to forgive you and support you during the crisis and you can reach heights you never before imagined."

Before the girl left my office that day, our discussion had turned from the sexual encounter in which she had been involved and toward what God would have her to do in life. She asked me about my own personal "calling" from God, and I told her that it had not always been clear. I told her that I sought God's leadership day by day, sometimes struggling to squint my eyes as I looked at a blurred path, other times elated over the brightness and crispness of a road completely in focus.

I shared with the girl a couple of portions of the Scripture which had meant much to me in my quest to seek God's will and not dwelling on past mistakes and failures: "Jesus replied, '. . . I will only reveal myself to those who love me and obey me. The Father will love them too, and we will come to them and live with them' " (John 14:23). "He will keep in perfect peace all those who trust in him, whose thoughts turn often to the Lord!" (Isa. 26:3). We cannot live abundantly in the present unless we have a healthy attitude pertaining to the past.

I talked with a married woman who had been involved sexually with a man other than her husband. The affair had lasted for over a year, but when she spoke with me she had broken-off with the man. It was over, but, in her words, "not forgotten." In reply to my question as to whether or not she was a Christian, the woman said, "I *think* I'm a Christian. I *try* to be." She went on to add, "I *hope* my sin is forgiven." Oh, the folly of such frustration!

If Christ is in a person, the person, without a doubt, is a Christian. Christianity is not a case of one *trying* to imitate Jesus' philosophy and life-style. Rather, it is inviting Jesus into one's life and letting Jesus live through the person. "Jesus said, 'When I come back to life again, you will know that I am in my Father, and you in me, and I in you' " (John 14:20).

The woman with whom I talked was a Christian if she had truly invited Christ into her life to live through her. By the same token, she was forgiven if she truly was sorry for her transgression and if she sought God's forgiveness. "Be kind to each other, tender-hearted, forgiving one another, just as God has forgiven you because you belong to Christ" (Eph. 4:32).

As we view our pasts with healthy attitudes and accept the forgiveness that God offers us, we must adhere to the biblical concept of forgiving others. Time and time again, the Bible makes it clear that we cannot really recognize the forgiveness of God unless we also forgive: "Your heavenly Father will forgive you if you forgive those who sin against you; but if *you* refuse to forgive *them, he* will not forgive you" (Matt. 6:14-15). "But when you are praying, first forgive anyone you are holding a grudge against, so that your Father in heaven will forgive you your sins too" (Mark 11:25).

The past is choking thousands of people, killing their present and destroying their future. These people reflect daily upon their failures and the failures of others. Such reflections grow to become hatreds. They hate their failures and eventually themselves. They hate others' failures and eventually others. These are the people . . . I repeat . . . these are the people who are "living their lives in quiet desperation"—sometimes exploding with deafening frustrations!

Don't Live in Past Successes

"Warning" sign number three deals with ruts caused by success. It has been said that first successes, especially early successes, have led to the downfalls of a frightening number of people. God must have had this very rut in mind when he said:

> "Let not the wise man bask in his wisdom, nor the mighty man in his might, nor the rich man in his riches.
>
> "Let them boast in this alone: That they truly know me, and understand that I am the Lord of justice and of righteousness whose love is steadfast; and that I love to be this way" (Jer. 9:23-24).

Some of the most ineffective dramatic presentations I have ever seen staged have come upon the heels of outstanding presentations by the same drama troupe. One such example is clearly embedded in my mind. I had the opportunity to attend several area premieres of my musical drama, *The Clown*. In one such premiere, the group presenting the drama turned in an outstanding job. Building up to "white heat" intensity, they had studied, rehearsed, prayed, laughed, cried. They simply had become totally involved in the production by the time the premiere evening arrived.

The Spirit of the Lord was evident in the auditorium in which the presentation was staged. An audience of over one thousand people seemed to hang onto every spoken word and to become an integral part of each song. The Lord utilized that musical drama group in a tremendous way. People were led to Christ; people were drawn closer to their Savior and pledged to make him truly their Lord.

Two months later, I again had an opportunity to attend a performance of *The Clown* by this same troupe. This time, however, as soon as I walked into the auditorium, I was very much aware that something was "different." As the presentation began, I quickly realized the "difference." No "white heat" intensity had preceded the performance; no dynamic involvement on the part of the group was evident; the Spirit of the Lord had not been invited.

Following the presentation, the group was very much aware of what had happened. They had depended upon that initial successful performance to carry them through other performances. Such dependence can be extremely costly. Whether in dramas, football games, scholastic studies, occupations, marriages, or any other aspect of life, unwise handling of initial or early successes can lead to temporary or total failure.

Of course, the exact "white heat" intensity of a premiere performance of a play can never be recaptured in its entirety—just as a football team cannot remain on the same emotional level for each game—just as the "second honeymoon" can never really parallel the first.

At the same time, however, we can utilize initial successes as springboards to greater successes, rather than letting them serve as opiates which dull our desires and our subsequent thirst for higher, more rewarding goals. In the words of Fran Tarkenton, quoted in an earlier chapter: "That taught me one of the greatest lessons I have ever learned in life. I knew then I could never recapture that victory. I knew I had to press on to greater victories and greater achievements. That's how it should be."

Oh, how Satan loves to see people caught up in themselves and in their past successes while slowly dying in the present. At the same time, Satan also loves to observe how early success "turns the heads" of some people. Getting a taste of success, these people exhibit the ardor of animals obsessed. Their high-quality goals become merely goals of quantity. They get their attention so firmly fixed on the goals that their eyes are not upon God. Such, perhaps, was the case of Satan himself.

Some theologians claim that Lucifer (the shining one) was the greatest of God's heavenly creatures. Lucifer, at first, led others in glorifying God. Later, however, Lucifer wanted more for himself.

The results of such an obsession are recorded in the Bible: "How you are fallen from heaven, O Lucifer, son of the morning! How you are cut down to the ground—mighty though you were against the nations of the world" (Isa. 14:12).

Such mention of Lucifer was recorded in Isaiah when Babylon was accused of falling prey to the same rut. Lucifer became Satan (adversary); Babylon became a fallen power, a shadow of her former self. When we begin to taste secular society's definition of "success," we are in grave danger of turning away from God and meeting with eventual failure in the worst sense of the word.

David Livingstone, the great humanitarian and man of God, wrote in his diary on the last day of his life: "My Jesus, my King, my Life, my All, I *again* dedicate my whole self to Thee."

Our dedication to Christ must never cease. We must never become complacent nor apathetic toward God and the work he would have us do. Just as the story of Abraham Lincoln teaches that failures can lead to success, the story of Lucifer teaches that successes can lead to failure.

Don't Be Robbed by Fear

The fourth and final "warning" sign I erect could simply state: *Fear Ahead—Do Not Apply Brakes.*

Oh, the amount of unhappiness caused by people fearing to fail! Dreams have been shelved and become heavy with dust because their owners did not have enough courage to work for their materialization. The biblical Job learned that if a person thinks he will fail, he will fail: "For the thing which I greatly feared is come upon me, and that which I was afraid of is come unto me" (Job 3:25, KJV).

I read a newspaper account of a college football player who, with his team trailing by five points, dropped a pass in the end zone with only ten seconds remaining in the game. Following the defeat, disgusted with himself and thinking of quitting the team, the player confided in a reporter that he knew he was going to drop it.

He told the reporter that he had been wide-open the last two times they had run that particular pass pattern. "But I didn't tell anybody I was open," the player said, "because I didn't want it thrown to me." The coach, however, had noticed the lack of coverage on the player and had sent word to the quarterback to throw it to him. "I didn't want the responsibility," the player confessed in frustration.

We all have entertained fear in our minds; we have been tempted to "duck" responsibilities and, at times, have succumbed to such temptations. However, if it is God who is leading us toward the areas we tend to resist, then we are surely transgressing against our Lord and belittling ourselves. If we say to God, "I'm afraid I can't do it," he in return will answer, "I never asked you to do it. Rather, I asked you to let me do it through you!" And that makes all the difference in the world.

"Fear not!" God says throughout the Bible. He is telling us to get our minds off ourselves and off our thoughts of our inabilities to accomplish the tasks he has given us. "For God has not given us the spirit of fear; but of power and of love, and of a sound mind" (2 Tim. 1:7, KJV).

Pressures may arise and conflicts may surface, but if we obey God, through him our fear can be conquered. This again underscores the vital need to think positively rather than negatively. If we fear failure, if we waste our time and pollute our minds with thoughts of failure, the more likely it is that failure will come.

At times, it is smart to be ignorant. A person can know so much about the difficulties of obtaining a certain goal that he defeats himself in his mind before he even attempts to succeed. Rather than concentrating on the reasons a certain thing cannot be done, I prefer to concentrate on reasons why it can be done. A person should not support his fears by consciously substantiating them with mental footnotes. Franklin D. Roosevelt said, "The only thing to fear is fear itself."

If you insist that you cannot do a particular thing or reach a certain goal, it is very probable that you won't. It is likely, however, that you insist you cannot accomplish something only because you have never done it before. This, in a way, is similar to "living in past failures."

"I can't do it," a boy responded when I asked him to make a ten-minute speech at a banquet.

"Have you ever tried it?" I asked him, knowing from personal observation that he was capable of fulfilling the request.

"No," he answered.

"Then how do you know you can't do it?"

"I just can't," he replied.

"Would you like to do it if you could?"

"Well . . . yeah . . . sure," the boy said.

I smiled and then looked at him deliberately. "You can do it," I assured him.

"How do you know I can?"

"Because," I began, "I have noticed the various things you have done in the past. There's no doubt the potential is there. Now all you have to do is utilize it."

"I don't know . . . "

"Listen," I interrupted, "don't I usually plan good programs for banquets and other such events?"

"Yeah," he responded.

"Well, do you think I would be stupid enough to ask somebody to be on the program if I didn't know he could 'cut it'?"

The boy made the speech and received an enthusiastic response from the audience. The crowd's reaction spurred him on and now he is actively seeking and fulfilling other speaking engagements.

You will never know what you are really capable of doing if you are constantly afraid to give anything a try. So what if you do fail? We've already discussed the significance of failures leading to successes. Failures are part of growing and maturing and happen to the most brilliant and successful people. Show me someone who has never failed and I will show you someone who has never had the courage to attempt anything worthwhile.

Personally, I would much rather attempt something and fail than to never attempt it at all. It is a challenge to try things I have never tried before. If I were to just keep on doing only what I've done up to now, life would soon become boring. Just like everyone else, I need to be involved in a continuing process of change. One vital aspect of growth is for one to do things he has never done before.

Take a moment and think. Isn't there something you would really like to do but have never had the courage to attempt? Pray about it. Make sure it is in God's will. Then ask for God's leadership as you plan and work for its attainment.

You can do it!

7/Turning The Bad Into Good

Life is not as idle ore
But iron dug from central gloom,
And heated hot with burning fears,
And dipped in baths of hissing tears,
And battered with the shocks of doom
To shape and use.

Tennyson

Several years ago, there was a popular song entitled "Even the Bad Times Are Good." The essence of the song was that a certain guy was so much in love with a certain girl that when he was with her she turned the bad into good. This should be everyone's goal! If we can only fall in love with life and with Jesus Christ who makes real life possible, we can respond to crises and problems in such a way that we will grow stronger instead of weaker as a result of them.

Tennyson's lines correlate with these words of George Buckley: "Trouble is not spasmodic; trouble is chronic. It is not an occasional capricious interruption into the normal process of life. Trouble is life!" Buckley is so right. Daily, it seems we are all faced with problems of some sort, physical, emotional, financial, spiritual. And, at one time or another, we are all faced with an unexpected crisis of major proportions.

Not long ago I talked with a desperate man who had lost his job and didn't know which way to turn. A pastor friend recently told me of a crisis facing one of his church members who was informed that her child was suffering from an incurable disease. Each day we read of accidents which take the lives of people in the prime of life. I recently counseled with a mother whose twelve-year-old daughter was pregnant.

What can one do when these things happen? How can one best cope with a situation that strikes with such terrifying force that recovery appears impossible? Robert Burns, in an attempt to answer such a question, posed another question: "Why comes affliction but for man to meet and master, and make crouch beneath his feet, and so be pedestalled in triumph?"

Burns' lines serve as a stairway to lofty responses to low points of our lives, but our initial reactions to our crises are not usually so positive. The normal, common reaction is, "Why me? Why did this have to happen to me?"

The woman whose child had an incurable disease was initially shocked and confused. Then, in the hope that the doctor's verdict might be wrong, she took the child to several other specialists. When the other doctors supported the findings of the first doctor, the woman became extremely upset, attacking the judgment of the physicians, choosing to avoid the reality of the situation.

Psychiatrists tell us, and most of us know from personal experience, that no two people react exactly the same way to crises. Some, like the mother, do not accept the crisis as a reality. Others experience total defeat and seem to exist on a level somewhere between life and death, never recuperating from the traumatic experience. Hostility, guilt, self-pity, anger, personality disorders, or more distraught mental or physical ailments . . . these could be reactions to unexpected crises in our lives. In contrast, reaction to adversity can be positive and optimistic. "We know that all that happens to us is working for our good if we love God and are fitting into his plans" (Rom. 8:28).

The above Scripture quotation is not to be used as a "spiritual Band-Aid" to bind our deep wounds and release us from hurt. It hurts when a loved one dies. It hurts terribly. A few words cannot erase the pain felt by the mother of a twelve-year-old girl who is pregnant. To be without a job, unable to support his family, brings a man to his knees in agony. There, however, on his knees, he can begin the process of turning the bad into good.

When my father died, God did not tell me, "It is good." When my wife came home the other day, deeply hurt by the unkind, cutting words of another woman, God did not tell me, "It is good." I worked on a manuscript for over three years and then sent it to a publisher. The publisher kept it two months, then informed me that they were interested in publishing it, but would like for me to change some things in it. I discussed the revision with them and we came to an agreement. I rewrote the manuscript, sent it back to them. They kept it for three months, then returned it to me with the notification that they had decided it would not fit into their present publishing plans. God did not tell me, "It is good."

The point is: God does not tell us that all things that happen are good. However, he does tell us that if we trust in him and keep close to him in times of crises and tribulations, he will lead us to grow stronger instead of weaker. With God, even the bad times are good.

Faith is the ultimate support during trying times. Faith is walking into the darkness without a light and knowing that God is there, loving you, ready to lead you to greater heights.

I think now of a marriage which, indeed, seemed to be made in heaven. When the husband died unexpectedly, friends of the woman felt she would fall apart. However, they were surprised at the positive, optimistic reaction which occurred when the woman got over her initial shock. Eventually, the woman remarried, and this marriage relationship now appears to be even more wonderful than the first. It has opened new vistas for the woman and has introduced her to a career in which she excels.

Several years ago, a heartbroken girl who was a high school senior came into my office. The boy with whom she had been "going steady" for three years had ended the relationship and she felt her world itself had ended. Her tears were evidence of the seriousness of the situation to her.

"I know something of what you might feel," I told her. "I experienced a similar ending of a relationship." She looked at me, apparently surprised that I *had been there,* but probably somewhat glad that I was able to understand the emotion. "When we broke up," I continued, "it seemed to knock the props out from under me."

"Really?" she asked.

"Really," I replied, smiling. "But since that time, I have praised the Lord over and over that it happened."

"Why?" she asked.

"Why am I glad about the breakup?"

She nodded her head.

"Because," I said, "if it weren't for the breakup with that girl, I might never have met and married Jean."

She perked up. She hadn't thought about that angle. "I couldn't imagine you without Jean," she responded, reflecting upon the closeness of Jean and me and upon the many things the two of us enjoy doing together.

"The girl involved in my breakup was sharp, just as the guy you've been going with is sharp," I told her. "But I dated many other sharp girls after that, and I believe I ended up marrying the sharpest one of them all."

She smiled. She knew I meant it.

"Now you and this guy may get back together—who knows? However, if you don't get back together, think of all the possibilities ahead. College is going to be a whole new ballgame for you—with a whole new set of players!" This time she laughed a faint laugh as she smiled at the possible challenge.

We prayed together that day before the girl left my office, because prayer helps to put things in perspective, to give them meaning, as we share with God and seek his guidance. Of course, God utilizes people as he mends, rebuilds, and strengthens us when we face seemingly insurmountable crises. We should be available as living instruments of God to help others as others minister to us in our times of need.

But how can we, *by the Spirit of the Lord,* help others and allow others to help us? Practically speaking, how do we cope with crises and rise above them? Reflecting upon Tennyson's lines, how do we grasp our troubles and shape them and use them to benefit ourselves and to glorify God through his Son, Jesus Christ?

Psychiatrists, ministers, and concerned laymen have suggested that we can best triumph over tribulations and be available to God's leadership if we apply the "3 R's" to our lives. "Readin', 'rightin', and 'rithmetic?" you ask. No, not those "3 R's." I refer to *receptive, resourceful,* and *resurgent.*

Be Receptive

The first step in dealing constructively with adversity is to face up to it in a realistic way. In other words, receive it for what it is and "roll with the punch." This particular quality is demonstrated by the apostle Paul in a portion of his letter to the Philippians:

> "I have learned how to get along whether I have much or little. I know how to live on almost nothing or with everything. I have learned the secret of contentment in every situation, whether it be a full stomach or hunger, plenty or want; for I can do everything God asks me to with the help of Christ who gives me the strength and power" (Phil. 4:11-13).

While I was in the seminary and serving in my first church-related position as a minister of youth, the office phone continued to ring one day. I picked up the receiver since it was apparent that no one else was around. "Carl," the elderly lady on the other end of the line said, "I think my husband is dead."

Her words hit me like the proverbial "ton of bricks." I had been engaged in planning a youth hayride, trying to determine the number of hot dogs needed to be purchased and the amount of Kool-Aid Jean should prepare.

The lady was a very faithful and active member in the church. She and her husband lived with their son and daughter-in-law and three grandchildren. The entire family was a credit to Christ. But only then was I to learn just how much of a credit.

"I'll be right over," I responded to her request when she discovered that I was the only one around and that the pastor or minister of education and music could not be located. As I left the confines of my office and got into my car to drive over to the house, I prayed that God would help me to know what to do and say. This was the first time I had ever encountered anything of this nature. Little did I realize that God would use the elderly lady and her family to minister to me more than he would use me to minister to them.

When I arrived at the house, the elderly lady and her daughter-in-law were standing on the carport next to a car. Nearing the scene, I saw that her husband was under the car that was jacked up. I exchanged acknowledgments with the two women; what we initially said, I don't remember. But I do remember their telling me that when the lady's husband was called for lunch, he didn't respond. She came out to check on him and found him motionless, apparently dead as a result of a heart attack. The ambulance had been summoned and arrived shortly after I did. The man's son was on his way home from work.

As I reflect upon the scene now, I recall nothing that I said that day. I'm sure that whatever it was it was not in the least bit profound. But the reactions of those two women, and later the son, and still later the grandchildren who came in from school, are still indelibly etched in my mind.

No one cried. I mention this not to say there is anything wrong with crying, but to say I was deeply impressed by their composures. The death was quite unexpected even though the man was rather old, but the family did not seem to be shocked. The serenity on their faces revealed that they were prepared for his death. The only spoken words I now recall came from the elderly lady who looked down at her dead husband as the ambulance attendants placed him on a stretcher. A smile caressed her face which glowed with tiny, web-like wrinkles. She then looked up at me and said, "He knows the Lord."

The better we know the Lord, the more power we have to be receptive when crises arise. As I look back upon my first ministerial encounter with death, I realize that the elderly lady understood these words of Paul and shared her understanding with her family: "No matter what happens, always be thankful, for this is God's will for you who belong to Christ Jesus" (1 Thess. 5:18).

No one can escape humanistic pains, difficulties, and losses, but through Christ and the hope he offers now and forever, we can meet these conflicts head-on and turn defeat into victory. In *Hamlet* Shakespeare wrote: "When sorrows come, they come not single spies, but in battalions!" This is all the more reason we must constantly keep in contact with the Lord and truly realize the words of the psalmist: "God is our refuge and strength, a very present help in trouble" (Ps. 46:1, KJV).

Be Resourceful

When crises come and, by the grace of God, we are receptive to them, we then must take a long, lingering look at ourselves. We need to get our strengths and resources into focus so that we might make the most of the situation at hand.

My son, Carl "Two," came home from school one day and informed me that he was going to draw a flower as homework for one of his classes. He then went to his room to work on the project, and I resumed what I was doing prior to his sharing that piece of information with me. Later "Two" shared his drawing with Jean. "Why, Son," I heard her say, "that's a good tree—real good."

"*Tree?*" I said to myself as I overheard the comment. "I thought he was drawing a *flower.*"

"Carl," Jean called to me, "come see Two's tree. He did a good job."

I went into his room and, sure enough, it was a drawing of a tree—and a good drawing at that. After I had congratulated Two on the drawing, I asked him what had happened to the flower idea. And he explained.

The *tree* had begun as a *flower* planted in a grassy meadow, surrounded by hills and a clear blue sky and a winding stream. But as the drawing developed, the size of the flower appeared to be much too large in proportion to the setting in which it was placed. So, Two added some limbs to the flower's stem, added branch-like strokes to the bud, and colored the *tree* accordingly. Now that is being resourceful!

Years ago, I heard a story about a woman who cherished a beautiful white scarf which had been given to her as a gift from a missionary to India. One day the scarf was on her desk, and she became extremely upset when she knocked over a bottle of indelible ink which stained the scarf. A visiting friend with artistic capacities saw the woman's sorrow over what had happened.

"Louise," the friend told the upset woman, "if you will let me take the scarf home with me, I think I might be able to remedy the situation."

"But the ink is indelible," the woman replied. "It won't come out—no matter what you do."

"I know," the friend responded, "but I still believe I can help."

The friend took the scarf home with her and set about working on it with her brush and colors, utilizing the stain marks by amplifying the odd forms caused by the spill. Soon an exotic and beautiful design was painted onto the scarf, and its owner cherished it even more than ever. A resourceful individual knew how to handle a distressing situation!

Evanghelos Georgakakis is a name you will want to remember. Several years ago he was the top man of three-hundred-sixty candidates who took the bar exam in Athens, Greece. This fact, alone, is outstanding, but the circumstances behind the fact would lead one to believe it was an impossible accomplishment.

Georgakakis was blind, a disability he received as a result of a German land mine explosion in 1944. He also had an artificial right hand and only one of his fingers on his left hand had any sense of touch. Georgakakis used the tip of his tongue to read braille. He got through law school by tape recording and memorizing sixty thousand pages of legislation.

May we look at our lives? May we inspect our abilities? May we consider our resources?

As I conduct a personal inventory utilizing these three questions, and as I am ashamed and embarrassed at the sometime shallowness of my resourcefulness, I am helped as I read the words of the nineteenth-century clergyman, Frederick Huntington: "Sorrow is our

John the Baptist, clad in grim garments, with rough arms, a son of the wilderness, baptizing us with bitter tears, preaching repentance; and behind him comes the gracious, affectionate, healing Lord, speaking peace and joy to the soul."

Be resourceful. Taking things where they are and, through the leadership of the Lord, making the most of them—that's what it's all about. In a speech pertaining to facing crises, Dr. Louis Linn, a psychiatrist, put it this way: "The better you've done your homework as a human being—developed concern for others and the world about you, established a stable family life and kept open the channels for love and excitement—the more likely you are to meet the inevitable crises effectively."

Be Resurgent

Resurgent means to "rise again," to "get back up when you've been knocked down." Accomplishment after accomplishment has been built upon previous failures. Being "down but not out" is one of the greatest attributes one can possess.

The most memorable football game in which I was involved as a player was one in which our team was behind 25-6 going into the final eight minutes of play. We had to win the game in order to remain in the race for the conference championship. Needless to say, things looked bleak. Hope was still alive, however, as I took a hand-off from the quarterback, found an opening in the line, and scooted into the end zone with approximately six minutes left on the clock. The extra point was booted and the score was now 25-13. Then . . . well, let me dust off an old scrapbook and open it up for you. The following account was recorded in the *Jackson* (Tenn.) *Sun* newspaper:

> "An inspired bunch of Humboldt High Rams rose to superb heights last Friday night to pull an almost certain loss out of the fire and edge a strong, highly-favored Jackson Golden Bear eleven by a 26 to 25 one-point margin, with barely seconds remaining on the clock . . .
>
> "In as dramatic a finish as you will see in many a moon,

> the Rams were behind two touchdowns with less than four minutes to play . . . and here is how it happened in those last four minutes . . .
>
> "Quarterback Jerry Williams sent Carl Mays straight down the field where Williams threw the speedy Mays a strike at the 25-yard line. One Jackson man hit him solidly on the 20 but slid off as Mays refused to be denied. He hit paydirt with three minutes and 27 seconds remaining in the game. Still, Humboldt trailed 25-20.
>
> "Playing the game to the hilt, the rams successfully tried an onside kick . . . Humboldt covered the loose pigskin . . .
>
> "With 48 seconds remaining, Humboldt picked up a first down at the Jackson nine.
>
> "A play into the line netted one yard. A pass fell incomplete. Nothing daunted, Williams tried again, a sharp rifle shot down the line to Mays in the flat. Once again Mays was hit immediately, but shook off his would-be tackler and zipped into the end zone with the winning points and pandemonium reigned."

We all have moments we like to relive in our minds—moments in which we rose above seemingly insurmountable odds to taste the sweetness of victory. These moments may come as we reflect upon a particular game or, more importantly, as we reflect upon the vital aspects of life itself.

Beethoven rose above deafness to compose majestic music. Milton defeated blindness to write words of depth and beauty. Helen Keller, who could neither see, hear, nor speak for a long time, achieved a victory that few people can ever imagine. This is what *resurgence* is all about.

Louisa Mae Alcott was told by an editor that she had no writing ability and should forget about attempting such endeavors. When Walt Disney submitted his first drawings for publication the editor told him he had no talent. At twenty-one years of age, F. W. Woolworth was not permitted to wait on customers in the store where he worked because his employer said he did not have enough sense to meet the public.

If, in the onslaught of crises, we truly seek God's leadership and say to ourselves, "With God's help I can," the victory we seek is about half won. If we are maturely receptive to the crises, if we pool our resources, if we work vigorously to win, then the other half will form completeness.

It seems that we do our most effective work in times of great struggle. That is why "come-from-behind" games are dramatically won in the last few seconds. That is why history can record the feats of people such as Beethoven, Milton, Helen Keller, and others. That is why the apostle Paul could write:

> "I have cheerfully made up my mind to be proud of my weaknesses, because they mean a deeper experience of the power of Christ. I can even enjoy weaknesses, insults, privations, persecutions and difficulties for Christ's sake. For my very weakness makes me strong in him" (2 Cor. 12:9-10, Phillips).

Prior to the above portion of Paul's letter to the people of Corinth, he told them of some of his experiences which were great enough to tempt anyone to boast about them. Then, he went on to say: "Because these experiences I had were so tremendous, God was afraid I might be puffed up by them; so I was given a physical condition which has been a thorn in my flesh, a messenger from Satan to hurt and bother me, and prick my pride" (2 Cor. 12:7-8).

It was Paul's belief that God allows us to face crises, disappointments, and frustrations so that we will be reminded that ultimate joy is not found in *things* or *people.* Paul teaches that abundant living is based not upon money, popularity, health, or our relationships with other people; it is based upon the relationship one has with God through his Son Jesus Christ. Such teaching amplifies the words of Jesus when he said: "I am leaving you with a gift—peace of mind and heart! And the peace I give isn't fragile like the peace the world gives. So don't be troubled or afraid" (John 14:27).

It is through his muscles' resistance to weights that a weight-lifter develops his body. In isometric exercises which build up the body, one set of muscles is briefly tensed in opposition to another set of muscles or to an immovable object. It is the struggle of muscle against weight or muscle against muscle that leads to increased power and strength. In our daily lives, we have the opportunity to expand and develop as humans and sons and daughters of God as we struggle against problems or crises that confront us.

You can do it!

8/Good—Gooder—Goodest

Happiness resides not in possessions and not in gold, the feeling of happiness dwells in the soul.

DEMOCRITUS, 420 B.C.

One sultry summer day I stopped off at an ice cream parlor to quench my thirst and to satisfy my longing for something sweet. After inspecting the ice cream flavor chart on the wall, I decided on a double-dip of chocolate chip. I got in line to await my turn to order.

In front of me was a woman with three boys. They had already made their requests and the girl behind the counter was generously fulfilling these requests. Having piled one of the cones high with strawberry cream, she walked to the counter and handed it to the first little boy. He took a big bite out of the ice cream and turned toward the other two boys with the words, "Hmm, this is *good!*"

Soon, the girl returned with a cone of chocolate ice cream and gave it to the boy who was second in line. Like the boy before him, he thanked the girl and immediately took a big bite of his treat. He was able to make an even larger dent than had the first boy. "Hmm," he said as he forced down the gigantic swallow and faced the other boys, "this is *gooder!*"

Shortly, the third little boy stepped to the counter and received his cone of what appeared to be cherry ice cream. Not to be outdone by the other two, he opened his mouth wide and bit into the cream. A red circle framed his lips and tipped his nose as a broad smile sprang upon his face. "Man," he told his companions in no uncertain terms, "this is the *goodest!*"

The good, the gooder, and the goodest—that's what this chapter deals with, because there are very few things which have a fixed value. The seemingly important things become trivial and the seemingly trivial things become important by the mere shifting of circumstances.

In Shakespeare's *Richard III*, the king is self-satisfied and seems to have everything he wants or needs. However, when his palace is besieged and his very life is threatened, he utters the line: "A horse! a horse! my kingdom for a horse!" In this one line he is saying that he will give up everything he once held so dear—his gold, his power, his prestige—for one, single, solitary nag on which he might escape.

As a young boy I saw a movie about some men who devised plans to go to Africa to find some diamonds and thus become rich. As the movie began and progressed, the men flew from New York and arrived in Africa where they lied, cheated, stole, and killed to get to the mines and the diamonds. They found the treasure, stuffed it into bags, and left the mines as multimillionaires. Making their way from the mines to the mainland, however, the men became lost in the jungle. They depleted their water and food supply and became desperate. Finally, they came upon some "natives" and began attempting to convey to the natives that they would give them all the bags of diamonds if the natives in return would only give them some food and water.

As a minister of youth I sat in my office one day and listened to a brokenhearted father tell me of his desire to "reach" his son, to communicate with him. "For years I've spent eighteen hours a day working to give my family everything they've needed or wanted," the man told me. "I'm rich. You know that. But I'd give it all up—the home, the cars, everything—and I'd be willing to struggle financially, if I could only gain Jimmy's respect."

With these three illustrations in mind—the king willing to swap his kingdom for a horse, the diamond hunters willing to swap their millions for food and water, and the brokenhearted father willing to sacrifice all his material wealth to gain his son's respect—I pose the question: What is good, gooder, and goodest to you? Or, more correctly, what is good, better, and best?

I pose this question because as we seek victory in life, our most difficult choices lie not in choosing between the good and the bad. Rather, our most difficult choices lie in choosing between the good and the best. That is why it has been said: The *Good* is the enemy of the *Best*.

In the biblical account as recorded in Luke 10:38-42 (Phillips), we can see an outstanding illustration of man's unfortunate habit of letting the good things of life get in the way of the best things in life:

> "Jesus came to a village and a woman called Martha welcomed him to her house. She had a sister by the name of Mary who settled down at the Lord's feet and was listening to what he said. But Martha was very worried about her elaborate preparations and she burst in, saying:
>
> 'Lord, don't you mind that my sister has left me to do everything by myself? Tell her to get up and help me!'
>
> But the Lord answered her:
>
> 'Martha, my dear, you are worried and bothered about providing so many things. Only one thing is really needed. Mary has chosen the best part and it must not be taken away from her!' "

Jesus did not grant Martha's request that Mary leave his side and come out into the kitchen to help prepare the big meal in which Martha was so involved. But Jesus' actions came not because Martha was engaged in "bad" things and wanted Mary to join her. Rather, he reprimanded Martha because she allowed minor things to take a major place. In other words, Martha was saying that Mary had too much to do and should not allow her time to be taken up by Jesus. Martha was saying that the "good" meal was more important than fellowship with Christ. Martha was saying that Mary should exchange her chance for potential spiritual growth for an opportunity to help prepare an impressive, prestigious meal.

So it is with many professing Christians today. We often get so wrapped up in so many *good* things in life that we have no time for the very *best.* And it is this misplacement of priorities that leads to mediocrity and failure rather than victory.

In John Bunyan's *Pilgrim's Progress*, there is a character named "Mr. Facing-Both-Ways." This man strives to "do his thing" and to "do God's thing" at the same time. This man wants to live a gloriously happy, committed Christian life. Needless to say, the character becomes filled with worries and anxieties as the *good* part of him fights with the *best* part of him—like Martha.

Good Things Cause Anxieties

Martha's actions robbed her of her peace of mind. And, oh, the number of us today who lack true peace of mind as a result of being involved in so many *good* things. I think now of an attractive Christian woman who is currently seeing a psychiatrist and is being treated for ulcers because she is doing so many *good* things. She is involved in this club and that club; she is raising money for this cause and that cause. It could be that she might be able to discard the psychiatrist and the ulcer treatments if she would "get out of the kitchen" and spend more time "at the feet of Jesus."

I think now of a beautiful teenager who could have offered so much to Christ—and to herself—if only she had had the time. She was a cheerleader (which was good), a member of the County Teen Board (which was good), a featured soloist in the school choral group (which was good), president of the Beta club (which was good), and she participated in several other worthwhile activities.

This girl's family and the people of her community were shocked when she died from a drug overdose. Her doctor later revealed that she had been a "bundle of nerves."

The girl had become strung out on *good* things. She had never paused to examine her priorities and to give her time and herself to the *best*. She had attended Sunday morning worship services in the church where she was a professing Christian and she did go to Sunday School, but this "touching base" type of religion did little to relieve the anxieties which multiplied as increasing *good* things continued to push the *best* from her life.

Like this girl and the woman before her, we all experience anxieties. We worry. As humans we cannot totally eliminate our tensions and concerns. As a matter of fact, some stress and strain is healthful and normal. It leads us to exercise caution and care before making decisions and it protects us from avoidable harm. But it is the *excessive* anxieties which destroy peace of mind and sometimes lives.

Jesus said: "So my counsel is: Don't worry about *things*—food, drink, and clothes. For you already have life and a body—and they are far more important than what to eat and wear" (Matt. 6:25).

Most people who read this book do not really worry about *things* in the sense to which Jesus was referring to the people of that day. Most of us are not worrying if we are going to have enough food to prevent our starving. We are not concerned that we will not have clothing enough to protect us from the weather or shelter enough to keep us warm and dry. Usually, our contemporary worry is egocentric. True, we worry about *things,* but the *things* about which we worry are not things of necessity. Rather, they are *things* which are important to our self-centered pride.

Let's face it—most of us want more to make us happy than we really need or deserve, and, at the same time, we are not grateful enough for the many things that are ours to enjoy. We want more than we need, whether it be in material wealth or in the prestige and pride resulting from good works.

An acquaintance of mine would thoroughly enjoy playing tennis regularly. He wants to learn to play better. But he doesn't want anyone to watch him learn. Therefore, he refuses to really get involved in the game. He is more concerned about making a fool of himself in front of people than he is in developing into an accomplished tennis player. So it is with Christians.

Much anxiety in the lives of Christians is caused by divided devotions. We are guilty of standing between *the joy of Christianity* and *things,* reaching and hoping for both and never being satisfied by either. Many of us cannot really get into Christianity and become "accomplished" Christians because our time and efforts are so concerned with doing things to inflate our self-centered egos or to please other people. God warned all mankind of this particular danger when he said: "You may worship no other god than me" (Exodus 20:3).

Jesus tells us that a person's "heart" will always be where he has his treasures. This means that a person's life-style will be determined by his priorities. One's wishes, desires, aims, goals, and ambitions will be centered in the "good life" or the "best life." The choice makes all the difference.

If one chooses the *best life*, he will discover that most of his worries will soon disappear and that God will lead him in dealing with the few that remain. As mentioned in earlier chapters, it is a case of allowing God to guide us into proper perspectives.

According to scientists, a dense fog which covers approximately eight city blocks to a depth of one hundred feet is composed of less than one glass of water. So it is with our "dense blanket of worries." If we only concentrate on the *best life*, our worries which appear to be so enormous can be squeezed into a small glass and dealt with intelligently.

Psychiatrists inform us that most of our fears never happen. They say that we anticipate the worst and, therefore, our fears are bountiful. These clinicians reveal that only about ten percent of our worries have any practical basis. That means that approximately ninety percent of our worries are pure fog with no substance at all. If we strive for the *best life*, God will lead us through this fog.

God will assist us in looking at our fears and eliminating those that have no practical basis for being. He will turn a mirror upon our self-pity. A reduction of one's self-centered ego will turn his mind away from himself and help him get a better focus on his troubles. Best of all, God will assist us in getting rid of the conditions which give birth to unfounded worries.

Good Things Cause Conflicts

Martha's actions caused her to attack her sister Mary. Martha was so engrossed in good things that it upset her for Mary to "waste her time" with the best. Martha was blinded by her choice of priorities. Such blindness causes conflicts. Such conflicts split a man and cause him to fight with himself. These conflicts split marriages, families, churches, communities, and nations. These conflicts come to mind as I read Jesus' declaration: "I have come to set a man against his father, and a daughter against her mother, and a daughter-in-law against her mother-in-law—a man's worst enemies will be right in his own home!" (Matt. 10:35-36).

Jesus does not want such conflicts to exist, but he knows they will as long as we continue to choose the good over the best. These conflicts and resultant attacks are as old as recorded history. Cain attacked and killed Abel because Abel worshiped God while Cain was caught up in self-worship. Jesus was attacked and killed because the pious religious leaders of the day had a form of worship which conflicted with Jesus' idea of the best. Later, Romans attacked and killed Christians who said the good life could never equal the best. Today, non-Christians and nominal Christians attack those whom they commonly refer to as "fanatics."

A sixteen-year-old boy made an appointment with me and came to my office. "I don't fit in anywhere," he told me. He went on to explain that since he had become a Christian a short while ago, his old non-Christian friends laughed at him and put him down. At the same time, the youth of the church he had joined thought he was a religious fanatic because he was taking his newly-found Christianity so seriously.

There was a very popular Sunday School teacher in the youth department of a church. In fact, she was so popular that many youth skipped the other teachers' classes to attend her class. This presented a problem and the problem had to be looked into.

As the situation unfolded, it seems that this attractive, magnetic woman was running a combination "Ann Landers Clinic and Glamour Course" on Sunday mornings. The girls were advised on proper makeup techniques and other charm secrets and found a listening ear as they revealed how they were misunderstood and mistreated by their parents, boys, and other humans.

No doubt, this woman was making Sunday School an attractive place for these girls to come. She caused it to be the popular thing to do. But these searching girls were drawn to the good things she offered, while rejecting the best things the other teachers offered. Her class majored on self-glorification which appealed to non-Christians and spiritual babies. Her popular class utilized no Christian literature, no Bible, while the other teachers were striving to make their classes Bible oriented. These teachers were attempting to "sit at the feet of Jesus" while the other woman was "in the kitchen." There, she was winning the conflict and the majority of the youth.

In tears, a young wife told me that her husband despised the church and everyone connected with it. She said that he was not a Christian when they had gotten married, but that she had hoped to lead him to Christ. That was three years ago and the leadership had proved to be unfruitful.

"He is more against Christianity now than he was when we were engaged," she told me.

As I now recall that young wife's words and tears, I think of the many conferences in which I have underlined Paul's warning: "Don't be teamed with those who do not love the Lord" (2 Cor. 6:14). I can think of no worse way to begin a marriage than for one partner to be aiming for the good life while the other partner is aiming for the best life. Such partners may share the same house and bed, but in reality they are miles apart. God tells us, "You may be sure that your sin will catch up with you" (Num. 32:23), and the wisdom of this admonition is greatly exemplified in the lives of people who choose husbands and wives without seeking God's leadership and guidance on the matter.

Good things cause conflicts. To some degree, we all have experienced such conflicts and have been hurt by them. Some of us have been hurt more than others; some of us are suffering at this moment. Thus, the important question is: How do we overcome conflicts and squeeze from them the victory we seek? As we consider answers to this question, I would like to share with you the experience of a young lady from a small southern town.

Joanne was a beautiful girl born into a family of low income. She jumped at the chance to marry the son of the town's wealthiest businessman. For the first four years of marriage, the couple enjoyed the good life. Thereafter, the "goodness" wore off and the husband sought additional thrills from other beautiful women.

The husband had never had to work; things had been handed to him. But the "goodness" of this also wore thin. To drown his frustrations and growing feelings of inadequacy, he increased his social drinking to the point of alcoholism. The floundering marriage continued to sink and divorce came. The husband's family supported their son and used Joanne as a scapegoat, blaming her for their son's downfall. With shrewd lawyers, the wealthy family turned the wife out with a minimum income. But she and the three children she now had were able to exist on the available finances which supplemented the income from the job she acquired.

Things became worse for Joanne, however, when three years later her former husband's parents were killed in an accident. It only took the former husband two years to deplete all his financial resources. The child support and alimony were stopped because they were simply not available. The former husband left town and Joanne added a part-time job to the regular job in order to support the children and herself.

Joanne's debts began to accumulate and later snowballed when one of the children had to undergo expensive surgery and remained in the hospital over an extended period of time. Later, the child died. The former husband was contacted, but he made no reply and did not return for the funeral.

At this low point in Joanne's life, a local church came to her aid. The church helped her to begin her climb out of debt and encouraged her to make a comeback. And come back, she did.

Joanne worked twelve hours a day and went to school three hours in order to gain a better job. All the while, she gave as much of herself to her children as she possibly could. She rededicated her life to Christ, renewed her determination to obtain the best life had to offer, and reflected upon the past only in order to help herself plan her future more wisely.

Joanne's smile of younger years returned and she regained the wonderful sense of humor she had possessed. Her additional study and hard work led to her becoming news editor of the newspaper for which she had begun as a girl Friday years earlier. Three years later, the new pastor of the local church moved to town. He was a widower and began to date Joanne shortly after his arrival. It wasn't long before they were married, joining lives and families to serve God and to work together to claim the best that life has to offer.

Joanne gained true joy, true victory, not as a *result* of good things, but *in spite* of good things. She rose above the depths to which the good life had taken her. She overcame conflicts by developing an attitude toward Christ, other people, and the world which led to victory. Her life became a living testimony that happiness and victory do not hinge on pleasant surroundings and circumstances.

As Joanne fell from the good life to bad times and then began her rise to the best life, she discovered that happiness and joy and victory are found in the quiet simplicities and fundamental virtues of life. She learned that victory consists of inward things that eventually determine outward circumstances, rather than it being outward circumstances that eventually determine inward things. Jesus said, "The Kingdom of God is within you" (Luke 17:21), and that is where real victory is found.

We can learn from Joanne's experience. If we permit outward circumstances to control our lives, we are doomed to failure. We must begin within and work outwardly, rather than begin from without and work inwardly. Our daily attitudes must not depend upon such things as the actions and reactions of the people around us or upon the circumstances which confront us. If we allow such a dependence to occur, we become no more than human mirrors reflecting our surroundings. Like chameleons, we will become like our environments instead of leading our environments to become like us.

Joanne, seeking the best, got to the point where she concentrated upon what she had rather than upon what she didn't have. She became receptive, resourceful, and resurgent. She epitomized the attitude credited to a pupil of the great teacher and preacher Dwight L.

Moody. It is related that Dr. Moody once offered a prize to the student who could come up with what he considered to be the best thought. This took the prize: "Men grumble because God put thorns with roses; wouldn't it be better to thank God for putting roses with thorns?"

Good Things Rob Us of the Best

Jesus Christ, the Son of God, was sitting in Martha's home, but she didn't have time to speak with him! Afforded the opportunity to reflect upon the situation, it is easy for us to see the folly of Martha's actions. But we need to focus upon our own lives and evaluate our own time priorities. I believe that it was just such an inspection and evaluation that led Paul to write: "Everything else is worthless when compared with the priceless gain of knowing Christ Jesus my Lord" (Phil. 3:8).

Choices. That's what life is all about. God has endowed each of us with the basic ability to make choices. This truth is so aptly exemplified in the account of Adam and Eve. God could have allowed us no choice in things. He could have created us as robots, programmed to always do what he would have us to do. But this is not the way God works and we are not mere puppets to be manipulated on strings.

We have the privilege to choose the bad, the worse, or the worst, just as we have the privilege to choose the good, better, or best. The spectrum is large; the choices are many. That is why on a scale of one (worst) to six (best), so many people tend to be satisfied, but unhappy, with less than the best. I know that I have been guilty of this very thing, and my guilt was solidified one day as God led me to read these words addressed to me and to others like me:

> "I know you well—you are neither hot nor cold; I wish you were one or the other! But since you are merely lukewarm, I will spit you out of my mouth!
>
> "You say, 'I am rich with everything I want; I don't need a thing!' And you don't realize that spiritually you are wretched and miserable and poor and blind and naked" (Rev. 3:14-17).

One evening as my family and I sat at the dinner table, eating and watching the TV news, my son vied for my attention. "Dad . . ." he began.

"Shh!" I cut him off as I listened to the newscaster tell of a tragic multiple-killing.

"But, Dad . . ." he began again.

"Not now," I interrupted, intent upon exactly how the murder was committed.

"I told two friends about God today," he quickly injected, unable to keep it to himself.

Guess who felt small enough to climb onto his plate and hide behind a green pea?

In essence, I had been telling my son that I was too busy with things of the world to listen to him. That, in itself, was bad enough. But to compound the wrongness of the situation, I was refusing to let him share with me an experience pertaining to God.

That simple but profound encounter at the dinner table led me to ask myself how often I had been guilty of such misplaced values. I looked into my life to see just how often I had been so concerned with less than the best. The inspection was terrifying. Using the words of an avid sports fan, I could have shouted, "I wuz robbed!" However, it wasn't merely a game in which I had been robbed. It was my life, and I had been robbing myself of my Lord's companionship.

This personal evaluation triggered by the dinner table encounter could not have come at a better time. Things had not been going very well for me. I had been involved in some conflicts which had led me to a depression of sorts. Ideas for writing and speaking were not flowing as freely as they had in the past. It was at this time that God allowed me to come to the aid of a black woman stranded on a busy interstate highway.

I saw the large, heavyset woman standing on the side of the highway, frantically waving her arms at the motorists who seemed to ignore her. Beside the woman stood a smaller female with a tentative, wide-eyed look upon her face. The companions, obviously chilled by the cold December wind, were several yards in front of a motionless car.

I passed the pair, swerved over to the side of the road, and rolled down my window. In my rearview mirror I saw a jubilant, flashy smile spreading across the face of the larger woman as she bounded toward me. "Praise the Lord!" she shouted as she neared the open window. "I didn't think anybody was ever gonna' stop!"

"What seems to be your trouble?" I asked.

"Outta gas," she replied, "Just plain ole outta' gas."

She asked me if I would take her to the nearest service station and I said I would. She and her companion got into the car and we made our way back into the traffic. The large woman talked with my wife Jean as I focused my attention upon the trucks and cars barrelling down the highway. Her small friend remained silent.

"Something told me not to pass up that last gas station," my heaviest passenger said to me, seeing that I was now in control of the traffic situation. Then, unexpectedly, the smaller friend broke the silence she had held.

"That *something* was the Lord," she said in no uncertain terms, "and you didn't listen to him. So he let you just run out of gas!"

What a parable!

Like the heavy black woman, I had not been listening to the Lord. I had been too busy, too involved, caught up in the good things of life. So the Lord, knowing that I couldn't get the best out of life on my own, was just letting me run out of gas!

It's when we run out of gas that we seek help. We think of the opportunities we had to refuel and we could kick ourselves for passing them by or letting them pass us by. We tell ourselves that if we can just manage to get out of the terrible situations that we have got ourselves into, we will never let it happen again.

I was "just plain ole running outta' gas." Unresolved conflicts were siphoning my gas and keeping a heavy foot on the accelerator at the same time. I was beginning to lose the vibrancy of life in the present and the expectancy of life in the future. But that's what happens when we spend too much time "in the kitchen."

A new commitment has occured in my life and I strive to refuel it daily. At times, I may become sluggish, and, for various reasons, need to get a tune-up. But may I never be guilty again of "just plain ole running outta' gas!"

Victory Is Free

Christ rejected Martha's attitude, but he accepted Mary's. Mary listened to him. She took her eyes off the good life and turned them upon the best. From Christ, she received what she could never lose. And all that she received was free. Happiness, joy, victory—these things cannot be purchased by any amount of money or by any amount of things. Yet, they are available to everyone. For Jesus tells us: "I have been standing at the door and I am constantly knocking. If anyone hears me calling him and opens the door, I will come in and fellowship with him and he with me" (Rev. 3:20). Victory is free. But each person must exercise the intelligence to accept it for himself. No one else can receive it for him; victory is never forced upon anyone. To live a victorious life is simple, but it takes a wise person to do it. Such contrasting simplicity and wisdom must have been on the mind of Thoreau when he wrote: "I am convinced from experience that to maintain oneself on this earth is not a hardship but a pastime, if we will live simply and wisely. Most of the luxuries, and many of the so-called comforts of life, are not only dispensable, but positive hindrances to the elevation of mankind."

The story of Francis of Assisi exemplifies the epitome of one who turned his back upon the good things in life in order to receive the best. The son of a rich merchant, he renounced his wealth to gain more from life. Even though he died in 1226, his words of wisdom still ring true today: "The eagle soareth very high, but if she had tied a weight to her wings she would not be able to fly very high; and even so for the weight of earthly things a man can not fly on high."

You can do it!

9/Enjoy Yourself!

"This is the day the Lord has made. We will rejoice and be glad in it" (Ps. 118:24).

Victory in life comes when one is at peace with God, with oneself, and with others. It consists not in having or doing, but in being. Continuous victory is not based upon temporary pleasures. To the victorious person, however, the small, daily pleasures are more meaningful than those fragile enjoyments experienced by the person who has not found victory. To the victorious person, the large pleasures become larger, while the person without victory all too quickly discovers such treats to be empty and short lasting.

Many psychiatrists tend to agree that the greatest amount of depression is experienced by people during holiday seasons—especially during Christmas. The depression comes as a result of people expecting much but getting comparatively little in return. These people expect the pleasures they receive to lead to happiness and victory, unaware that victory is never based upon such treats. These people are unaware that it is victory itself that leads to a greater satisfaction from high-quality pleasures, whether these pleasures be small or large.

It has been said that pleasure is a single musical note, while happiness or victory is an entire symphony. With such an understanding of the difference between the two, it is easy to see why a man without victory in his life could be discontented on a 'round-the-world vacation trip, while a victorious man could find fulfilling enjoyment at home watching television with his family. At the same time, the victorious man would have the capacity to derive great enjoyment from the romantic 'round-the-world vacation, while the other man would be unhappy in front of the TV at home. A person's surroundings merely provide the setting, not the basic plot.

People who have much money and who are always doing "things" can be miserable, while people who have comparatively little money and who do a minimum of "things" can be fantastically happy. Or, vice versa. Material "success"—or the lack of it—seems to have little bearing upon whether or not one is victorious. Material "success"—or the lack of it—may certainly alter one's life-style to some degree, but will have little bearing upon the basic person "underneath" it all.

Thomas Jefferson wrote in 1788: "It is neither wealth nor splendor, but tranquility and occupation, which give happiness." I agree with Jefferson because tranquility is found in God, and one's most satisfying occupation is found through following God's leadership. There is no happiness apart from God and no truly rewarding occupation apart from God's leadership.

God calls us to a victorious life: a life filled with highs and lows, mountains and valleys, pleasures and crises. This chapter offers practical suggestions on how to enjoy better the high-quality pleasures which can add to the fullness of a Christian life.

Set Definite Goals

"I can't wait till tomorrow!" my son overflowed enthusiastically on Christmas Eve. His eyes shot out sparks of light and it was easy to see that it would be difficult for him to get to sleep that evening. In his mind, he could see himself surrounded by new toys and candy and surprises. Eager anticipation seemed to dominate his very being. Such an anticipation is not a bad thing to have.

Each of our days can be much more enjoyable and satisfying if we can live each day in anticipation. Such anticipation is made possible if we set definite short-term and long-term goals and work toward reaching and enjoying these goals.

Unless we are working toward definite goals, we cannot realize the potential enjoyment that is ours to have. Like my son on Christmas Eve, we all become excited over anticipating things we desire. It is the looking forward to things that makes life itself so exciting. True, the Christmas season becomes a season of depression for many because their shallow anticipations are unfulfilled when the pleasures they receive do not give them what they expected to obtain. But through God's leadership, the victorious person can set and obtain goals which are eventually as satisfying as they are exciting.

All victorious Christians set goals to glorify Christ in their lives while on earth and to meet Christ face-to-face when their earthly lives are completed. These same people should determine exactly what they are going to do in life to accomplish the goal of glorifying Christ and to give that face-to-face meeting more meaning.

Depression is a major ill in our society. We all have experienced it, some more than others. But the victorious person can overcome temporary depression when he realizes that depression comes as a natural result of not having anything to look forward to. It also comes when a person looks too far ahead at his seemingly unreachable long-range goals and forgets about the need of daily, intermediate, short-range goals. I know what I am talking about here, because I have been guilty of "looking too far ahead" more times than I would like to admit.

Now, to some degree, I have learned to "demagnify" the largeness of my "impossible dreams" by setting and obtaining more reachable goals on my way to larger, more difficult ones. It seems to me that I am not really getting the most each day has to offer unless I'm working toward a certain thing and seeing tangible results of that work. True enjoyment is within my grasp when I know I am effectively utilizing the talents and abilities that are mine.

The businessman reaches long-term goals as he obtains daily goals; the career woman realizes her life-long ambition as she conquers daily mountains; the father becomes a successful father not all at once, but little by little, day by day; the mother and wife accomplishes her dreams of what a home should be, slowly, daily, as she patiently enjoys reaching small goals which lead to larger ones.

As a teenage athlete, I set a goal for myself to do one hundred pushups each evening prior to going to bed. I began the initial evening with ten pushups, later advanced to twenty-five, then to fifty, seventy-five, and finally on to one hundred. It was a long time coming, but daily goals and weekly goals cut down immensely on the impossibility of the eventual goal.

Just as one needs to set and reach goals of personal accomplishment, one needs also to look forward to special "treats." Reflecting on my childhood, I recall the afternoons in elementary school being more bearable as I looked forward to going to the grocery store on the corner near my home. Each day, I was allowed to stop at the store on the way home from school to get a soft drink and a bag of peanuts. I would always take a swig of the drink to lower its level in the bottle, then I would rip open the bag of peanuts and pour the peanuts into the bottle. Then, having shaken the contents of the bottle well, I would join some of my friends on the grassy bank in front of the store where we settled the problems of the world.

No matter if I had a good day or bad day in school, the grocery store visit was always eagerly anticipated. Work around the house or seemingly long homework assignments may have been on the agenda for later, but the soft drink and peanuts made such tasks less imposing.

Today, knowing I must be working toward some personal accomplishment in order to reach my potential enjoyment, and knowing that I still enjoy "treats," I always try to fill my days with much of the former and at least a little of the latter. After a satisfying day of work, the enjoyment can be capped off with the anticipation of a family get-together or a ball game or a TV show or a movie or a certain meal or some other form of entertainment that does not defile Christian principles.

Of course, we cannot always regulate our daily schedules. We cannot always accomplish certain goals exactly when we want to; nor can we always be "treated" as we would like. But in order for our enjoyment potential to be reached, we should realize we must work toward definite goals; this is a necessity. And we should fully realize that "treats" are icing on the *cake of life*—especially to the person who has already tasted victory.

Take One Step at a Time

I recall hearing a story about a man who got into his car with his family to go on a vacation trip. They lived in New York and were going to drive to California. Everyone was all packed and ready to go, but the man just sat motionless behind the steering wheel. When his wife asked him why he was not starting the car, he turned to her and told her that he was waiting for all the traffic lights between New York and California to turn green. Stupid, huh? At times, however, we are guilty of such stupidity.

Most of us have failed to begin something because of the many obstacles or "red lights" that seemed to be in front of us. So, we decided to wait until all such lights were green. The man who was going from New York to California would get to his destination by taking the traffic lights one at a time. If we follow suit, if we take obstacles or "red lights" one at a time, life will be much more enjoyable and we will find ourselves accomplishing tasks that once seemed to pose problems.

We need to anticipate the future with eagerness, but, at the same time, we need to live our lives day by day. In recent reading, I discovered that "Day by Day," the popular song from the musical *Godspell*, obtained its words from a prayer written by Richard of Chichester in the thirteenth century. It is a prayer with which he began each of his days. If we could sincerely utter the same prayer as we seek enjoyment from each day of our lives, the enjoyment would have a better chance of being ours:

"Day by day, day by day,
O dear Lord, three things I pray,
. . . to see thee more clearly
. . . to love thee more dearly
. . . to follow thee more nearly
day by day."

As I was driving down an interstate highway one evening, on my way home from a speaking engagement, I turned on my radio and immediately picked up the voice of a man reading something entitled "Just for Today." I was captivated by what he said and quickly pulled over to the "emergency only" shoulder of the highway and wrote down the address he shared with those who would like to obtain a free copy of the brief message by Dr. William S. Hendrie.

I think it is appropriate that I, in turn, share this with you:

JUST FOR TODAY: I will try to live through this day only, and not tackle my whole life's problems at once. I can do something for twelve hours that would appall me if I felt I had to keep it up for a lifetime.

JUST FOR TODAY: I will be happy. This assumes to be true what Abraham Lincoln said, "Most folks are as happy as they make up their minds to be."

JUST FOR TODAY: I will try to strengthen my mind. I will study. I will learn something useful. I will not be a mental loafer. I will read something that requires effort, thought and concentration.

JUST FOR TODAY: I will adjust myself to whatever is, and not try to adjust everything to my own desires. I will take my "luck" as it comes, and fit myself to it.

JUST FOR TODAY: I will exercise my soul three ways. I will do somebody a good turn, and not get found out. I will not show anyone that my feelings are hurt; they may be hurt, but today, I will not show it.

JUST FOR TODAY: I will be agreeable. I will look as well as I can, dress becomingly, talk low, act courteously, criticize not one bit; not find fault with anything and not try to improve or regulate anybody except myself.

JUST FOR TODAY: I will have a program. I may not follow it exactly, but I will save myself from two pests, Hurry and Indecision.

JUST FOR TODAY: I will have a quiet half-hour all by myself, and relax. During this half-hour, sometime, I will try to get a better perspective of my life.

JUST FOR TODAY: I will be unafraid. Especially, I will not be afraid to enjoy what is beautiful: and to believe that as I give to the world . . . so the world will give to me.

Take one step at a time and live one day at a time. Such stepping and such living can lead to a full, complete, enjoyable life. After all, a successful life is nothing more than a long line of successful days. A person's entire life can be changed when he begins changing his days, one by one. Time is relative. Some people can accomplish more in one day than others can in a whole week. Some people can find more enjoyment in one day than others can in a lifetime.

Form Good Habits

As a teenager, I enjoyed and participated in sports, especially football, baseball, and basketball. It was fairly obvious when I was in the seventh grade, however, that I would probably never be very tall. So, when I chanced to see a movie about the "Harlem Globetrotters" and marveled at the ball handling ability of one of their players, I decided to devote much time to work on my dribbling, passing, and "moves" with the ball. The following year, when the local high school coach saw my desire and progress, he called me aside one day to give me some encouragement and advice. That day, he told me something that I have never forgotten—something which I have repeated to sports teams, drama troupes, choirs, and others working to accomplish certain tasks.

"Carl," the coach said, "practice doesn't make perfect." He paused for effect as I hung onto every word he had spoken. Then he continued with, "*Perfect* practice makes perfect."

He was a smart coach. He knew that a person could spend literally years practicing on something, but if the person practiced incorrectly he would never obtain the goal for which he was striving.

Our daily habits determine who we are and what we are. Our

daily habits determine what goals we set. Our daily habits determine what we achieve and what we fail to achieve. Rabbits produce rabbits. Chickens produce chickens. Acorns produce oak trees. And everything we do or think produces its kind in our lives. In the words of Emerson: "You cannot do wrong without suffering wrong; nor can you do right without being rewarded for it. The reward is contained in the act itself . . . and therefore must be of the same nature."

It may sound trite, but it is so true: A person gets out of life exactly what he puts into it. Page after page of the Bible outlines the basic areas in which man forms bad habits and suffers from these habits. Misdirected habits lead to excessive pride. Immature habits produce envy and jealousy. Distorted habits result in hate. Slothful habits give birth to destructive idleness. Frustrated habits leave one open to gluttony. Obsessive habits yield greed. Perverted habits bring about lust. On the other hand, the products of positive habits are positive. Such is the lesson from the Bible; "A man will always reap just the kind of crop he sows!" (Gal. 6:7).

Work habits, eating habits, recreational habits, thought habits, study habits, spiritual habits . . . these are among the things which lead to victory or failure—to enjoyment or boredom in life.

Be Enthusiastic

It's Tuesday afternoon as I write this. My son, Carl "Two," stayed up past midnight last night completing his homework assignments. It seems all of his teachers chose the same evening for heavy doses. When I went into his room at seven o'clock this morning to awaken him, he didn't appear to be too enthusiastic about the idea.

"Two?" I called him as I switched on the light.

No answer.

"Time to rise and shine," I said as I walked to his bed and flipped back the covers.

He groaned.

"Up!" I said.

He groaned again, turned over and looked up at me through slits.

Beady eyes from deep recesses threw daggers. If looks could kill . . . .

"Do I have to?" he moaned.

"Up!" I answered.

"Five more minutes . . ." he plead, "just to rest my eyes . . . ."

"Up!" I answered.

I mention this incident now, because it was only a short time ago that this same boy, no matter how hard he tried, could not get to sleep on Christmas Eve. The excitement was too much for him, but he did finally manage to get to sleep somewhere around two A.M.—after having tossed and turned in bed for what to him seemed like days. However, at five-thirty A.M., he was by my bed, shaking my arm, telling me it was time to go down to the Christmas tree. He was bright-eyed and bushy-tailed, looking as if he had awakened refreshed from a long winter's nap. Enthusiasm bubbled from within.

What is the one word which describes the change in his attitude about arising early after getting to bed late? The word: *Motivation.*

Motivation is the term which simply describes whether or not we are enthusiastic about something. If we are motivated to do something, we will jump into that something with energy to spare. If we are not motivated to do a certain thing, the enthusiasm and resultant successful achievement will not be there.

Many newspaper "want ads" pertaining to job openings begin the description of the type of person wanted with the words, "Must be self-starter." This, of course, means that the person must be able to motivate himself or herself to do a particular job or to sell a particular product. In life, we all should be "self-starters" if we are to experience the inherent joy that is ours for the taking. But "self-starters" are made, not born.

We become enthusiastic about something when we think about it enthusiastically. It gets back to the principle that we are the products of our thoughts. Thoreau lived in a world very similar to the world in which we live. During his lifetime, there were robberies, killings, rapes, illicit sex, crooked politicians, hypocrites, wars, racial strife, and many forms of social injustice that upset him. He had the same type of daily problems that most of us have; he experienced small annoyances and large crises. But upon awakening each morning, this man would lie in bed and think of all the *good* things he could think of. Such thoughts would lead to enthusiasm, and he would soon jump up from his bed, self-motivated to live life to the fullest.

If we practice being enthusiastic about things, even when we don't feel like being enthusiastic, enthusiasm will come. As Shakespeare indicates in *Hamlet*, "Assume a virtue, if you have it not." It was this bit of advice that led Edwin Booth, one of the greatest actors in the history of the American theater, to decide that he would never permit himself to assume any ungraceful attitude, even when he was alone. As a consequence, Booth is said to have had the epitome of unconscious grace on stage. His *stage presence* was tremendous.

Our *enthusiasm presence* can be tremendous if we will not let ourselves be without enthusiasm, even when we are alone. If we continue to act enthusiastic about life and all that life contains, we will become enthusiastic. The more we become enthusiastic about the victorious life, the more we will enjoy the life and bask in the victory that is ours.

This idea of "thinking enthusiastically" is not to suggest that we be phony or assume a head-in-the-clouds "Pollyanna" attitude. Rather, it is to suggest that we be real—that we thank God for victory—that we be counted among those who are glad to see the roses in the thorns instead of being disgruntled over the thorns in the roses.

Norman Vincent Peale has described enthusiasm as "faith that has been set afire." Thoreau stated, "None are so old as those who have outlived enthusiasm." Emerson said, "Nothing great was ever achieved without enthusiasm."

Great enjoyment can never be ours unless the vital quality of enthusiasm is inherent in our daily lives.

Think Big

Driving through a small town, I saw on the window of a vacant store some graffiti which caught my eye. "A Big Shot," the graffiti began, "is a Little Shot who kept on shooting." I like that. Another line I like is "Attempt something so large that unless God intervenes it will fail."

The "Big Shot" advice reminds us that it is imagination, dedication, and just plain old hard work that eventually pays successful dividends. The "Intervention of God" aspect underlines the fact that nothing truly great is ever accomplished by man alone; the partnership of man and God is behind all worthwhile achievements.

Many people are not experiencing true enjoyment in life because they either lack "shooting power" or they leave no room for God's intervention. If one shoots too low, he may find that his life is rather boring, even though he may be reaching his goals. Most basketball fans are aware that because of the height of contemporary players there has been some talk about raising basketball goals from ten to eleven feet to make the game more exciting and interesting. Such raising of goals in our lives can add the same positive qualities.

We all should pause at times to evaluate where we are in life, where we have been, and where we are going. If one's plans and dreams are too small, it is more than likely that he is missing out on excitement, accomplishment, and daily energy. He may be trying to "play it too safe," or he may be failing to attempt something that can succeed only with God's help.

The bigger and better our goals, the more of ourselves we will use. Shooting high requires more utilization of our abilities and talents. People who waste their abilities and talents are frustrated and unfulfilled as persons. These people can never know the real meaning of enjoyment.

Setting and reaching big goals does not necessarily mean obtaining money and "things." It seems our society has always been attracted to the "rags to riches" stories of people who began with a few pennies and turned the pennies into fortunes. Such people should be commended for their imaginations and hard work, but we should not set them up as the epitome of what happiness and enjoyment are all about.

I personally know some "low-goal-oriented" people who are financially rich. Had they shot higher, they may not have been rich now, but they would have more enjoyment, excitement, and interest in life. I personally know some "low-goal-oriented" people who are financially poor. Had they shot higher, they probably would not be poor now, and they would have more enjoyment, excitement, and interest in life.

How big are your thoughts? If you have big thoughts, you have to grow as a person in order for these thoughts to become realities. If you have small thoughts, you can remain small.

A personal inspection might reveal that the goals you have set for yourself and God are much too low. If this is the case, then take time to consider what all you and God could do. And don't be afraid of failing. If you follow God's leadership, you will never desire something that is beyond your accomplishment. God doesn't work that way. He never taunts us with goals that are unobtainable for us. Hudson Taylor, founder of the China Inland Mission, put it succinctly when he said: "God's work, done in God's way, will never lack God's supply." The Bible puts it even more succinctly: "Jesus said, 'Anything is possible if you have faith' " (Mark 9:23). "For God is at work within you, helping you want to obey him, and then helping you do what he wants" (Phil. 2:13). "For I can do everything God asks me to with the help of Christ who gives me the strength and power" (Phil. 4:13).

"Thinking Big" applies to all aspects of life—spiritual, occupational, family, and other areas in which we are involved. Many times, however, people who are giant thinkers in one area are midget thinkers in other areas. Pity the poor man who is big in business and little in family. Consider the miserable man who is large socially and small spiritually. Think of the unfortunate man who is really into spiritual matters, but who disassociates such matters with his relationship to other people. There are distorted "big and little" people throughout our society—people who are lopsided and thus unable to experience the enjoyment which could be theirs.

If one pauses to evaluate the size of his dreams and aspirations in the various areas of life and finds himself lacking, he should be challenged to grow. At the same time, he should determine he will be happy where he is as he sets his sights on higher levels. That does not mean he should be satisfied with where he is. Rather, it means that when his eyes are opened to his shortcomings, he should begin to enjoy each level to the fullest "on his way up." Realizing he is going to grow now, he should not "wait to be happy" when he arrives at where he determines he should be. The eventual happiness and enjoyment will be multiplied tremendously if he makes the best of the climb and enjoys the struggle. The struggle, the climb, and the growth will be more rewarding if one adheres to the advice of Goethe: "One ought, every day, at least hear a little song, read a good poem, see a fine picture, and if it were possible to speak a few reasonable words."

Practice Humility

"Those who think themselves great shall be disappointed and humbled; and those who humble themselves shall be exalted" (Matt. 23:12). History reveals to us the outcome of people who exalt themselves—who think primarily or only of themselves and what they are going to get out of something. Time and time again, these men and women have been humbled and brought to their knees. I think of the Herods, the Pilates, the Hitlers, the Napoleons, the Dillingers, the Al Capones, the "Bonnies and Clydes." I also think of people who are relatively unknown to the world but who are well-known in the communities in which they live; these are people who think the world revolves around them and for them.

In these same communities, however, we have sincerely humble people whose thoughts and actions say about them all that needs to be said. It was people such as this to whom Jesus referred when he said: "Humble men are very fortunate . . . for the Kingdom of Heaven is given to them" (Matt. 5:3).

In my experience in working with people, it seems that it is invariably the relatively quiet, soft-spoken people with generous but unassuming attitudes who really get the jobs done and who really enjoy life. These people do not actively seek recognition, credit, and applause for what they do, but, more often than not, they receive it. They do not seek "high places," but their deeds often take them there. These people, at some time in their lives or after their deaths, become exalted. Gandhi, the past leader of India, epitomizes such people. This man sought only to find freedom and peace for the inhabitants of his country. He gave himself to help others and, while doing so, became a model of one who exemplifies humility and brotherly love.

Those who seem to never get the jobs done and who never really enjoy life are those who are preoccupied with themselves. They show little consideration for the feelings of others. They show little sensitivity or tact. They tend to dominate public meetings and private conversations, and their favorite word is "I." Such people need to realize that their unhappiness is caused by their own attitudes towards themselves and others. Such people need to reflect upon the wisdom of these words penned by Emerson: "A great man is always willing to be little. He has gained facts, learns his ignorance, is cured of the insanity of conceit."

Not long ago, I talked with a woman whom I shall call Mrs. Smith. Mrs. Smith was bitter because, in her words, "Everybody takes me for granted." She said that her husband and children showed no appreciation for her cooking and housecleaning and other general tasks she did for them. I didn't know the woman's family and maybe they did lack in their appreciation for her, but it was evident to me that her attitude was not helping the situation.

After I spoke with Mrs. Smith, a middle-aged woman, I thought of my own mother and of the many years she did the same type of tasks for our family. I can never recall my mother seeking a show of appreciation, but she received it—more and more as the years passed. To me, no self-pity or bitterness was evident in her life, nor is it now with her husband dead and all her children grown-up and living in their own homes. She never looked upon her work as something to be repaid by praise. Rather, she looked upon it as something she did for her family because she loved her family.

Even now, when all of her children return for a visit, she bends over backwards to do things for us, no matter how much we may protest that she is doing too much. Still, as in the past, she never seeks credit for what she does, but, as in the past, she receives it. That's the way it is, I guess. Credit comes when we do not seek it. Adulation never comes to those who ask for it.

I spoke recently with a young married woman who told me that her mother constantly reminds her of all the sacrifices she made for her. "Whenever my mother is around me," the young woman said, "she says things like: 'After all the diapers I pinned on you, the least you can do is . . . .' " The mother is too mentally blind to see that she is driving her daughter from her, rather than winning appreciation from her daughter.

This mother, like Mrs. Smith, is not experiencing the joy that humility can bring. They are too busy seeking praise and appreciation for such rewards to be theirs. On the other hand, however, there is such a thing as "false humility" and such a thing as "going overboard on humility." So, maybe we should ask ourselves, "What exactly is humility and how far should we go in humbling ourselves?"

In answer to this compound question, I take this opportunity to share with you these thoughts:

"Humility is to have a right estimate of one's self—not to think less of himself than he ought" (Spurgeon).

"True humility is not an abject, groveling, self-despising spirit; it is but a right estimate of ourselves as God sees us" (Tryon Edwards).

"Humility is the genuine proof of Christian virtue. Without it we keep all our defects; and they are only crusted over by pride, which conceals them from others, and often from ourselves" (Rochefoucauld).

"He that places himself neither higher nor lower than he ought to do, exercises the truest humility" (Colton).

"Humility is not a weak and timid quality; it must be carefully distinguished from a groveling spirit. There is such a thing as an honest pride and self-respect. Though we may be servants of all, we should be servile to none" (E.H. Chapin).

It seems that the quality of one's humility is in direct proportion to the satisfaction he is getting from his life-style. That is, the more one feels he is accomplishing something positive in life and utilizing his talents and abilities, the more he refrains from trying to prove to himself and the world that he is great.

A person needs to determine the type of life-style he wants to lead before commiting himself to any particular way of life. Education, occupation, marriage, and other related areas should not be hastily jumped into. For example, too many females get married, have children, and then later resent the fact that they have to be wives and mothers. Too many males get married, have children, and then resent the fact that they have to be husbands and fathers.

Because of unwise decisions made early in life, males and females are frequently pushed into life-styles and occupations they do not really enjoy. Later, when they determine what they would really like to do in life, the previously made decisions are seen as deterrents to their pursuits. Thus, come bitterness and dissatisfaction with life. Thus, comes the lack of humility in the lives of people who feel life has struck them a low blow, when actually the blow has been self-inflicted.

"Don't cry over spilt milk" is an adage which I have heard all of my life—and it certainly applies here. Or, as Paul put it: "No, dear brothers, I am still not all I should be but I am bringing all my energies to bear on this one thing: Forgetting the past and looking forward to what lies ahead" (Phil. 3:13).

In golfing terms, it is a case of "playing things as they lie." If a golfer makes a poor drive off the tee, he can't continue to dwell upon that initial shot and thus let the remainder of his game suffer. He must accept the shot as a poor shot and then concentrate on what he must do in order to make the best of the situation.

If earlier, unwise decisions are robbing you of present peace of mind, it might be best to take your eyes off yourself and your mistakes and place your eyes upon the people with whom you have been sharing your miseries. If you can exalt these people that you have been resenting, you, in turn, might be exalted. If you can only go about your daily tasks in the best manner possible and "play things as they lie," you may find yourself gaining enjoyments you never thought could be yours. If you can dedicate yourself to helping those around you, to being sensitive to their needs and aspirations, you will find yourself growing as a human being.

You may also discover that your "unwise" decisions were not so unwise after all—that only your negative attitude has been coloring the decisions and making them appear to be darker than they actually are. Remember, as a person matures, his or her ideas about things frequently change. And our attitudes have a lot to do with such changes. It was of such attitudes and such changes that Longfellow wrote when he penned these words: "I will be a man among men; and no longer a dreamer among shadows. Henceforth be mine a life of action and reality! I will work in my own sphere, nor wish it other than it is. This alone is health and happiness."

You can do it!

10/The Spirit Of The Lord

"But when the Father sends the Comforter instead of me—and by the Comforter I mean the Holy Spirit—he will teach you much, as well as remind you of everything I myself have told you" (John 14:26).

"I want to be happy, but I can't," a young woman said to me as we sat in my office. "I've tried, but I just can't."

I looked at the young wife, mother, and working woman. The frustration in her eyes revealed to me that she was in the same boat as many other young adults in today's society. She was trying her best to cope with contemporary pressures—to really live life rather than merely exist on a plane far below her potential. "No, you can't be happy," I agreed with her. A shocked, disappointed look sprang to her face, mixing with her already frustrated expression. "Not by yourself," I continued.

Then, I reached for my Bible and turned to Luke 1:34-35, and read: Mary asked the angel, "But how can I have a baby? I am a virgin." The angel replied, "The Holy Spirit . . . shall overshadow you, so the baby born to you will be utterly holy—the Son of God."

With a blank expression now registered upon her face, the young lady in my office looked at me, seeming to ask me, "What in the world does Mary's getting pregnant have to do with me?"

Before she could verbalize her question, however, I answered, "Similar to Mary, we could ask, 'But how can I have happiness and victory? I am miserable.' To this question, God answers, 'Victory can come to you through the ministry of my Holy Spirit.' "

So it is. It is the Holy Spirit who leads us to happiness. It is totally impossible to live a vibrant, victorious life apart from the Spirit of the Lord.

That day in my office, the young woman and I discussed the fact that there is more to Christianity than just making a profession of faith and having your name added to the church roll. We talked about the growth and maturation of the Christian. I told her that such growth and maturation is made possible by the same person who makes real victory or happiness possible, the Spirit of the Lord, known as the Holy Spirit.

Now, with this same concept in mind, I think it is only fitting that this book be concluded with a chapter pertaining to the Holy Spirit. For without such an emphasis, the previous chapters would have little significant value.

What—or Who—Is the Holy Spirit?

There are many misconceptions about the Holy Spirit. Some people claim that the Holy Spirit is an "it" rather than a "he." Such people say "it" is an *influence* coming from God and is not a *divine person.* However, when Jesus refers to the Holy Spirit, Jesus uses personal pronouns in his references. This is clearly seen in John 14:26. John 16:7-14 reinforces Jesus' view of the Holy Spirit as a person rather than an "it" power emanating from God.

In God's revelation of himself, God has definitely taught us that there is only *one* true God: "You may worship no other god than me" (Ex. 20:3). At the same time, however, he has also taught us that there are three persons in the Godhead—God the Father, God the Son, and God the Holy Spirit: "Therefore go and make disciples in all the nations, baptizing them into the name of the Father and of the Son and of the Holy Spirit" (Matt. 28:19).

The Holy Spirit has always been. Early, in Genesis 1:2, we are told, "And the Spirit of God moved upon the face of the waters" (KJV). As the Holy Spirit "moved" upon original matter, he brought forth its inherent potentials. Later, as he "moved" in the lives of numerous Old Testament people, he worked to bring forth their potentials. To them, he became the source of spiritual perception, of mental abilities, and, at times, of physical strength:

> "So as David stood there among his brothers, Samuel took the olive oil he had brought and poured it upon David's head; and

the Spirit of Jehovah came upon him and gave him great power from that day onward" (1 Sam. 16:13).

"The Spirit of the Lord God is upon me, because the Lord has anointed me to bring good news to the suffering and afflicted. He has sent me to comfort the broken-hearted, to announce liberty to captives and to open the eyes of the blind" (Isa. 61:1).

"At that moment the Spirit of the Lord came mightily upon him (Sampson) and since he had no weapon, he ripped the lion's jaws apart, and did it as easily as though it were a young goat!" (Judg. 14:6).

As these and other Old Testament Scripture passages indicate, the Holy Spirit was not constantly present in the lives of the believers in God. For special work and emphasis, he came and went, assisting people to seek and follow God's leadership and to find and develop their inherent abilities and talents. Later, as we inspect the New Testament period, we see that the Holy Spirit came upon Mary and that Jesus was born as a result (Luke 1:34-35). Still later, we find that the Holy Spirit came upon Jesus to work in his life:

"Then one day, Jesus himself after the crowds had been baptized, was baptized, and as he was praying, the heavens opened, and the Holy Spirit in the form of a dove settled upon him, and a voice from heaven said, 'You are my much loved Son, yes, my delight' " (Luke 3:21-22).

"Then Jesus returned to Galilee, full of the Holy Spirit's power" (Luke 4:14).

"And you no doubt know that Jesus of Nazareth was anointed by God with the Holy Spirit and with power, and he went around doing good and healing all who were possessed by demons, for God was with him" (Acts 10:38).

Then, as Jesus' earthly ministry in his physical body drew to a close, he told his disciples that he would soon be leaving them, but that the Holy Spirit would come and abide with them. With these words of promise, this chapter was opened (John 14:26). But, and this is very important, Jesus also said the Holy Spirit would *remain* in the lives of believers upon his coming:

> "If you love me, obey me; and I will ask the Father and he will give you another Comforter, and he will never leave you. He is the Holy Spirit, the Spirit who leads into all truth. The world at large cannot receive him, for it isn't looking for him and doesn't recognize him. But you do, for he lives with you now and some day shall be in you" (John 14:15-17).

This promise of Jesus materialized on that day referred to as "the Day of Pentecost":

> "Seven weeks had now gone by since Jesus' death and resurrection, and the Day of Pentecost had now arrived. As the believers met together that day, suddenly there was a sound like the roaring of a mighty windstorm in the skies above them and it filled the house where they were meeting. Then, what looked like flames or tongues of fire appeared and settled on their heads. And everyone present was filled with the Holy Spirit and began speaking in languages they didn't know, for the Holy Spirit gave them this ability" (Acts 2:1-4).

As the Holy Spirit came upon the believers in Christ, these believers were able to tell others about the mighty miracles of God. They conveyed the good news to people of various cultures—Parthians, Medes, Elamites, and people from Mesopotamia, Judea, Cappadocia, Pontus, Ausia, Phrygia, Pamphylia, Egypt, Libya, Rome, and other areas. Pilgrims had come from these places for Pentecost, the annual celebration fifty days after Passover. All of these people who heard of what God had done and was doing were amazed that these Galileans were able to speak so many languages (Acts 2:6-17).

What happened at Pentecost can never happen again; for there can only be one such initial coming of the Holy Spirit to fulfill Christ's promise. But there is no need for it to happen again. Christians today are still benefiting from that coming, because the Holy Spirit has remained in the lives of Christians for centuries and he still remains. It is as Peter said when he spoke to the amazed and bewildered crowd drawn to the Pentecost happenings:

> "Each one of you must turn from sin, return to God, and be baptized in the name of Jesus Christ for the forgiveness of your sins; then you also shall receive this gift, the Holy Spirit. For Christ promised Him to each one of you who has been called by the Lord our God, and to your children and even to those in distant lands!" (Acts 2:38-39).

Regardless of Jesus' promise that the Holy Spirit would come into the lives of *all* believers and in spite of the fact that Peter was given the authority to claim the Holy Spirit is available to *all* Christians, many people disregard the Christian universality of the Holy Spirit.

Upon the mention of his name, some people immediately are repelled, viewing the Holy Spirit as "something" appealing only to the unintelligent or the overemotional or the religious fanatic. People with such a view can never experience the real victory that could be theirs in life.

On the other hand, some people think that only the "spiritual elite," after much growth and sacrifice, have an opportunity to be "baptized by the Holy Spirit." Such selfish thoughts become barriers between these people and true victory.

Thinkers on either end of this wide spectrum, and all those thinkers somewhere in between, are grossly incorrect if they do not believe that the Holy Spirit is present in the life of *every* real Christian. This statement is upheld by Paul's teaching in his letter to the Christians of Rome and to all Christians:

> "Those who are still under the control of their old sinful selves, bent on following their old evil desires, can never please God. But you are not like that. You are controlled by your new nature if you have the Spirit of God living in you. (And remember that if anyone doesn't have the Spirit of Christ living in him, he is not a Christian at all.)" (Rom. 8:8-9).

Paul's teaching supports the point so clearly made previously by Jesus and Peter: that the presence of the Holy Spirit is a necessity in the lives of Christians, rather than an added ingredient for only a relatively few. And it is this presence of the Holy Spirit in our lives that makes it possible for our lives to be happy, enjoyable, victorious. It is through the work of the Holy Spirit that the positive concepts, attitudes, thoughts, and actions suggested in the first chapters of this book can be effectively applied to our lives. The Holy Spirit is God with us and in us.

The Holy Spirit "Changes" Us

It is the Holy Spirit who leads us to see that our frustrations in a "winless" life are the result of our being separated from the God who created us. It is the Holy Spirit who reveals the fact that we have fallen far short of our potentials. He leads us to repent, to change, to have faith that God, through his son Jesus, will give our lives meaning now and eternally.

To "repent" means to "rethink." When we repent, we think of the totality of life in a new way. The Holy Spirit shows us how we have been wrong and how we can be right. He leads us to Christ and, thus, to God and to the "newness" of life: "When someone becomes a Christian he becomes a brand new person inside. He is not the same anymore. A new life has begun!" (2 Cor. 5:17).

Through the work of the Holy Spirit of God, we are turned around and set on a new path. This new path helps us to put things in proper perspective. We repent, and our attitudes change; our goals, ambitions, and aspirations become different from what they were previously. As we repent, we are "sorry" for the way we thought and lived in the past, sorry we went against ourselves, our fellowman, and, most importantly, sorry we rebelled against our God.

Taking a positive step in repentance, we are baptized with water to indicate that the "old things" have been washed from our lives. More importantly, however, we are baptized with the Holy Spirit who has led us to Jesus Christ and who now leads us in a new life-style as he shows us God through Jesus Christ. But the work of the Holy Spirit is not ended with this initial "conversion' experience.

The Holy Spirit "Ministers" to Us

After having led us to Christ, the Holy Spirit helps us grow and mature as Christians. He helps us obtain the joys and victories that can be ours. He ministers to us, meeting us at our points of need and filling us with life in the areas in which we have been lifeless. That is why Jesus told his apostles: "When the Holy Spirit, who is truth, comes, he shall guide you into all truth, for he will not be presenting his own ideas, but will be passing on to you what he has heard. He will tell you about the future" (John 16:13).

As the Holy Spirit ministers to us, he guides us to the truth—if we seek his guidance and if we seek the truth. Life-changing decisions do not have to be made on our own if we will only invite the Holy Spirit to lead us in the decision-making process. Our finite minds cannot comprehend infinite wisdom, but such wisdom for decision-making can be ours if the Holy Spirit is in control of the situation. Paul said: "I advise you to obey the Holy Spirit's instructions. He will tell you where to go and what to do, and then you won't always be doing the wrong things your evil nature wants you to do" (Gal. 5:16).

What causes unhappiness, frustrations, winless lives? Paul himself gets down to the nitty-gritty of such predicaments and says that the basic cause is due to our refusing to listen to the Holy Spirit. In Galatians 5:19-21, he tells us that disobedience to the Holy Spirit results in impure thoughts, lust, idolatry, spiritism, hatred, fighting, jealousy, anger, complaints, criticisms, envy, murder, drunkenness. In his words, without the guidance of the Holy Spirit, there exists a "constant effort to get the best for yourself . . . the feeling that everyone else is wrong except those in your own little group . . . ."

Simply speaking, in contrast to the negative attributes, the Holy Spirit seeks to bring out the best that is in us; he seeks to cultivate our inherent potentials. The Holy Spirit comes into a person's life at the time of his conversion. If the person allows the Holy Spirit to grow in his life, then this person will mature as a Christian. This Christian maturation will be marked by the "fruits of the Spirit" and the person will be equipped with the "gifts of the Spirit": "When the Holy Spirit controls our lives he will produce this kind of fruit in us: love, joy, peace, patience, kindness, goodness, faithfulness, gentleness and self-control" (Gal. 5:22-23). "Now God gives us many kinds of special abilities, but it is the same Holy Spirit who is the source of them all . . . . It is the same and only Holy Spirit who gives all these gifts and powers, deciding which each of us should have" (1 Cor. 12:4,11).

The Holy Spirit "Comforts" Us

Jesus called the Holy Spirit the *Comforter*, the *Paraclete*, meaning "the one who stands by our side." In good times and bad times, his companionship looms large. He is no "fair weather friend." And, since he is the Comforter that Christ promised to his apostles when it became necessary for Christ to depart, we can reasonably expect that the Holy Spirit's comforting will be Christ-like.

Being Christ-like, the Holy Spirit is for us the presence of Jesus, just as he became the spiritual presence of Jesus for the apostles when Jesus physically departed from them. In this capacity, the Holy Spirit comforts us as he represents God the Father through God the Son. His work as the Comforter is varied: "The Holy Spirit helps us with our daily problems and in our praying" (Rom. 8:26). "His Spirit searches out and shows us all of God's deepest secrets" (1 Cor. 2:10). "For it won't be you doing the talking—it will be the Spirit of your heavenly Father speaking through you!" (Matt. 10:20).

The Holy Spirit Removes the Glass

As this book moves toward conclusion, I share with you the story of a small boy reared in extreme poverty. He never had a real, manufactured toy. His "toys" were sticks or boxes or some discarded junk he found and applied his imagination to. When he had the opportunity to go downtown, however, he would stand and gaze at the toys in the store windows. In his mind, the toys would become his and he would play with them and watch their movements and listen to their sounds, as they remained untouched, still and silent behind the protective glass windows.

Then, one day the small boy was involved in an accident and was rushed to a hospital. After initial examinations were made, there proved to be no serious damage, but the boy was in pain. To take his mind off the pain, one of the nurses bought him a small truck and brought it to him. As the nurse handed it to him and he reached wide-eyed to accept it, there was an extended silence. He then looked up at the nurse's wide smile as he caressed the truck. "There's no glass," he said in amazement. "I can touch it."

To many people today, life is out there somewhere—appealing, beautiful—but untouchable. They can see it; in their minds they can almost experience it. But frustrations and unhappiness grow as they continue to be separated from it by a thin barrier. If you are among these people, if you are longing to really live life rather than merely exist, it is the Holy Spirit who has the power to remove the glass and bring you into touch with the life that you know can be yours. "Touch life" with the power that is yours through the work of the Holy Spirit.

You can do it!

About Carl Mays

Carl Mays is the director of Creative Ministries, Inc. of Gatlinburg, Tennessee. He is also special group consultant for The Sheraton Gatlinburg Hotel and Conference Center. His ministry includes writing, speaking, performing, directing—giving full vent to his creativity.

A native of Tennessee, Carl is a graduate of Murray State University and New Orleans Seminary. He did additional graduate work at Memphis State University and served several churches as minister of youth.

Other books he has written for Broadman include: The Magic of J. B., Mr. Adams: A Parable for Parents and Others, *and* Celebration: A Writer in Search of a Play. *He has also made contributions to other Broadman releases. With other publishers, Carl has done a number of books and a recent musical,* The Clown.

He is married to the former Jean Berry, also a multitalented person. The Mays have one son, Carl "Two," who has inherited his talent from his parents.